Clay in the Master's Hands

John Frank

Clay in the Master's Hands

Second Edition

by
Donna Frank

Cock-A-hoop
PUBLISHING
TULSA, OKLAHOMA

Clay in the Master's Hands

Printed in the United States of America

99 98 97 96 95 5 4 3 2 1

Library of Congress Catalog Card Number: 95-068808

ISBN 0-9640706-2-6

Published by

Cock-A-Hoop Publishing
P.O. Box 4358
Tulsa, OK 74159-0358
918-747-4777

Distributed by

EFANEF Co.
P.O. Box 727
Sapulpa, OK 74067
918-224-6610

Edited by E. Andra Whitworth
Designed by Carl Brune

This book is dedicated to . . .

Grace Lee, who was his complement every step of the way, for it was she who was responsible for getting his products into the hands of the public with her artistry and salesmanship;

Joniece, my sister and best friend, who inherited from our father the gift of creating art that people want to live with.

Thirty spokes share the wheel's hub;
It is the center hole that makes it useful.
Shape clay into a vessel;
It is the space within that makes it useful.
Cut doors and windows for a room;
It is the holes which make it useful.
Therefore profit comes from what is there;
Usefulness from what is not there.

LAO TSU
Sixth Century B.C.

A C K N O W L E D G M E N T S

My special thanks and gratitude go to the members of the Frankoma Family Collectors Association for encouragement and support, both verbal and financial, that contributed significantly to the publication of this second edition.

PREFACE

In 1976 I was living at the beach in Venice, California, when I was approached about writing a history of my father, the business, and the family. I felt I was ready and welcomed the opportunity. I had been successful in publishing some travel articles, short stories, and a bit of supermarket trivia, but here was a chance to prove myself a "serious writer," as they say. I started to work soon afterward.

I made several trips to Oklahoma to gather facts, figures, and dates, after which I settled down to listen to all the taped interviews I had conducted with various people who were present during the early years when Frankoma's history was being made. But it turned out that, as cooperative and sincere as each of them had been, in the end all I had was a report of events from *their* points of view. So most of what I had from them were their *impressions* of what had taken place, and when I put them all together, a number of striking contradictions surfaced. Who was I to believe? The fact was, they were all true!

So the first decision I had to make was—should I record their impressions (whose and which ones), or should I write the book as I viewed the whole story from my eyes? Well, I had to opt for my own, not because I thought mine was in any way better, it was simply the more famliar route. I reasoned that as long as events and dates were as accurate as could be determined, perhaps my readers would be just as interested in knowing what it looked like from where I stood.

So there you have it. Please understand that, should you ask someone else, there's a chance you may get a slightly different version of the way a particular event unfolded. Just be reminded that's their view, not mine, and in the end, the game was necessarily "Author's Choice." Thank you.

In 1977, one year after I began work on the book, *Clay in the Master's Hands* was published and on the market. The first printing was out the door in no time at all and, in years to come, would be a valuable collectors item. And certainly no one would be more dumfounded by its popularity than its author.

When the first edition of *Clay* was written, it was a nice story and had a certain appeal to the generation whose parents had used Frankoma in their homes daily. But to them it was commonplace, and its presence was taken for granted.

Now, almost two decades later, there is a new generation, having grown up with fond memories of the love and appreciation their grandparents had for Frankoma. They have come to be very sentimental about those items they remember seeing and using as children when visiting the grandparents' home. Their own appreciation for those items as fine art pieces has grown with them, making them more avid collectors than any before them. Also realizing its collectability, previous generations are taking a second look and noticing the rising values of the older Frankoma pieces, and are joining the ranks of collectors in ever greater numbers.

And with this realization came into being the need for a second edition of *Clay in the Master's Hands*. This new generation of Frankoma collectors had more questions. They wanted to know more of its history. What were the stories behind what they had inherited or acquired? And where could they find more of the fine older pieces?

In September of 1994, the Frankoma Family Collectors Association came into being. I mentioned to FFCA members the possibility of expanding and updating the first edition. I had rather rushed the first one, omitting some information I later wished I had included and, as a result, I hadn't that sense of "completion" I expected, and needed. The basic story had been told, but there was more that needed to be said, questions to be answered.

There was immediate interest in my doing this (at the time primarily for the collectors' benefit) and, before I knew it, a special account had been set up to receive funds to back its publication. I was overwhelmed by the trust and generosity of so many wonderful members. Without them, you would not at this moment be holding this book in your hand.

I chose a publisher in whom I had confidence to advise me and who would work with me to produce a second edition I thought I could be proud of, and that collectors would be pleased with as well. Then I went to work immediately on the revisions.

In the meantime, the Frankoma Family Collectors Association has continued to expand and grow, not only in membership, but in its scope and purpose. As word spread about the organization, Frankoma collectors surfaced from every corner of the United States, and all wanted to become part of the Frankoma Family.

The Frankoma Family Collectors Association was chartered on January 31, 1995, John Frank's ninetieth birthday, which we believe would have pleased him immensely. It is now a national, non-profit, educational and social organization dedicated to the appreciation, preservation, and promotion of Frankoma Pottery as a collectible.

The ambitions of this group also include the raising of funds for scholarships to encourage budding ceramic artists, by holding auctions and selling various limited-edition pieces to be made for FFCA by Frankoma Pottery.

FFCA now publishes the quarterly newsletter, *Pot & Puma*, in addition to the *Prairie Green Sheet*, also published quarterly between issues of the regular newsletter. The latter deals primarily in the buying, selling, and trading of Frankoma collectibles, with ads free to members. Non-members may advertise at a nominal cost.

Each September is held what has come to be called a "family reunion," when the Frankoma collectors get together for two or three days to buy, sell, trade, socialize, and share their collecting experiences. Experts in various categories offer mini-seminars and are there to answer all related questions. Novice collectors learn from some of the more experienced about identification, colors, where and what to look for, values, dates of manufacture, repair, and much more. The reunions are in Sapulpa, but eventually will also be held in other cities throughout the U.S.

The reunion also offers opportunities to tour the Frankoma plant, and to visit the Frank home and other sites significant to Frankoma Pottery's history.

All are welcomed into the Frankoma Family. For membership information, write to FFCA, c/o EFANAEF Co., P.O. Box 727, Sapulpa, OK 74067. To join, simply fill out the application at the back of this book and mail it with a check for twenty dollars (annual dues) to Nancy Littrell, P.O. Box 32571, Oklahoma City, OK 73123-0771.

Donna Frank
May 1995

INTRODUCTION

This is a story about an ordinary man who became an extraordinary man because he dared to do what came naturally for him. And what was natural for him was to live his life in service to his Master by serving His people. Even the products he devoted his life to creating were an extension of his philosophy, as they were also designed to serve.

My father was an elemental but sage-like being. His message was put forth in pure and unadorned language so that anyone who would listen could understand. And that message was translated into physical form through the art he produced—simple in design and priced so that all could afford to live with and enjoy his products. In this respect, his message was also that of the Master's—no one shall be denied the joy of knowing beauty in life, if they truly desire it.

My father knew that the Master was always at his side. When he seemed to be talking to himself, he was merely talking things over with his Friend and asking for guidance. And he lived his life as an example of how to know the abundance that is rightfully ours when we make the choice to become as clay in the Master's hands, and let Him make of us what He needs us to be in order to serve.

I was urged by my father to be a living example of what I say I believe. "After all," he often told me, "you're the only book some people read." In his lifetime, many people read the book that he was, and many were inspired to follow his example. No mere volume could ever be as effective as was his presence. But this story is written in the hope that, in his absence, the book that he was will continue to be read, even if only in printed form.

"It is said of John Frank that he was the kind of man small boys hope they'll grow up to be, and old men wish they had been . . ."

CHAPTER 1

When America was settling into the new twentieth century, the ability to feed one's family had little to do with determining the size of it, causing many families to remain quite poor. Adam and Marie Frank and their three children, Anton, Ruth, and Paul, lived in a small three-room flat in one of Chicago's poorest neighborhoods.

Adam was employed by the telephone company as an electrician. His salary was barely adequate to house and feed the five of them. It was no wonder that when John was born on January 31, 1905, it was less than a blessed event. But then came David and Josephine and Francis.

John was five years old when he was put on the street corner to sell newspapers. When the freezing winter winds became unbearable, he learned that if he shouted, "And they found the body! Read all about it!" the papers would sell quickly and he could go home with his quota and get warm.

John was no more than an average student in grade school. His clothes were inadequate to withstand the blustery Chicago winters, and he was often hungry. Although he was lacking in knowledge of history and geography and arithmetic, he was the teacher's favorite because he made for her gifts of pictures he drew of birds and trees and animals he found in the school library books. He was an exceptional student in art.

On his way home from school, he walked through alleys to gather scrap paper from the office trash cans on which to make his drawings. He especially liked to draw birds, and he began to learn all he could of the various species and draw each of them in intricate detail.

His mother, Marie (she pronounced it *May*-ree), watched proudly and encouraged him to draw other things as well. Many times she patiently sat while he drew her face; or sometimes he would sketch a kitchen scene with her standing at the washtub or sitting at the kitchen table.

When John was fourteen, only he and the three younger children remained in the household. The marriage of his mother and father had always been a stormy one, perhaps because they did not choose each other but were chosen for each other by their staunchly traditional, and probably well-meaning, German families. And now they were quarreling more frequently and more violently than ever. To add to the stress, one of his younger brothers was often causing havoc in the neighborhood and would disappear for days at a time.

John's artwork served as a refuge for him. It was a comfort to lose himself in a drawing of meticulous detail while shutting out the sounds of discord and lack of love around him.

It was the summer of 1919, and his brother Anton returned from the war. He began attending a nearby Church of the Nazarene, and John watched as Anton's bitter restlessness gradually changed to a calm acceptance. He adored Anton and longed to know the same confidence and peace that had settled upon his brother.

Anton's invitation to accompany him to a summer church retreat in the mountains was accepted with excitement and anticipation. John had been away from the city only once, as a young child, and he was enchanted by the scenery and wildlife. There were real live birds and flowers and trees, which to now had been only pictures in books. The air was clean, and the water sparkled with purity.

Having grown up in a large family, John had seldom been shown the love and attention he needed as a child. So the quality of fellowship and acceptance that he felt with the warm and caring people who gathered at the retreat was a whole new world for him, and he reveled in their company.

John and Anton stood together at the rear of the outdoor tabernacle at the last evening service. The minister said, "If you feel in your heart that the time has come for you to be born again to a new life of peace and joy, come forward and make your commitment. We welcome you with love."

John's decision was already made. Anton put his arm around the shoulder of the slender fourteen-year-old youth, and together they walked to the altar.

Young John openly and publicly dedicated his life to the Master and vowed to serve Him by serving His people.

At once he felt new energy flood into him, and he wanted to fly. So this was what it was like! The old falls away, and the new begins. Life now had new colors and dimensions and lightness. His life would mean something else from now on. He looked forward to going home and finding ways to serve.

During the night John awakened to hear the rain softly pelting the trees and foliage outside the dormitory. He walked out into the woods and stood looking upward, letting it gently splash his face.

"I know," he whispered. "You've sent the rain to tell me I've been washed clean."

The rain soon stopped, and the first light of morning appeared in the eastern sky, the eternal symbol of hope that accompanies every new day. "Give me all the tests You will, but I'll never become discouraged. You'll see how strong I can be. I promise to serve wherever You need me."

*C*hicago looked different to John now. No longer a loud and oppressive environment, it was now a city of potentially loving people who needed someone to care and help relieve the suffering. And John was so filled with the Spirit, he felt he could take on all of Chicago singlehandedly.

When his first year of high school was completed, he dropped out to help with the family income. His mother was heartbroken. No matter what privations they had to endure, she knew John was special and should go to school and become an artist. However, John's mind was rigidly set. The family needed him.

Adam managed to get his son a job at the telephone company. For one year, John climbed high ladders to clean and replace light bulbs in the huge Kellogg plant. The labor proved boring and unchallenging, as well as too strenuous. His body was thin, and he tired easily. His mother persuaded him to return to high school and earn his diploma.

Adam and Marie then moved their family to another neighborhood, where John would have the advantage of specialized art instruction at a better high school. He was tutored by an excellent art teacher who encouraged him daily and introduced him to new media of expression in art.

No longer was John limited to black and white pencil drawings. Now he was learning the techniques of painting with oils on canvas; the effects he could accomplish with the use of water colors; and the creation of hundreds of colors he never dreamed existed with mixtures of natural pigments. Colors excited him! Then he found something that would free him from the limitations of all those art forms that only allowed him expression in the flatness of two dimensions. John discovered a medium with which he could create in *three* dimensions, and it was also a medium that lured and challenged him to continue his experiments with a world of colors and color combinations. It was the introduction of clay that opened that door for him. He fell in love with clay. His imagination soared with all the possibilities it offered. And clay would change his life forever.

At his new school John became acquainted with a young man who invited him to a Salvation Army meeting. It seemed the young people he met there were alive with the same enthusiasm and high energy he was experiencing, and he knew he belonged. God had begun to direct him. He was where he needed to be, and he was ready to serve.

He learned that musicians were needed, and his father managed to buy him an old trombone at a pawn shop. John learned quickly and was soon playing in small groups on the street corners of Chicago. Music did not come easily through the oft frozen mouthpiece of the old horn, but the enthusiasm behind it somehow made it sound like music.

Out of his horn came *Onward Christian Soldiers* in the humid heat of summer, *Bringing in the Sheaves* in autumn, and at Christmas time there was *Oh, Come All Ye Faithful*. A few of the listeners got salvation, but almost everyone got hot soup and a piece of bread. The Salvation Army people knew they couldn't lead a soul to God on an empty stomach. And the tambourine jingled.

Many simply sat through a service as the polite price of a meal or to get in out of the cold. The Corps people knew it, and it was all right. They remembered to what lengths the Master had gone to save that one lost sheep, and someone would smile knowingly, drop another potato into the pot and say, "Praise God."

John went about so turned on to the joy of life that no one could be discouraged in his presence. His enthusiasm was contagious, and there were those who became members of the Corps because they wanted what he had, the magic that flowed in and around and through him that said,

John Frank. Chicago, c. 1921.

"Happiness is knowing the Master!" But there were always those who could not let go of the yesterdays that held their spirits earthbound. They were simply afraid to fly.

Others came alive when they allowed all of their yesterdays to be forgiven, looking forward with faith to today and tomorrow. And those also became ignited with the fire that urged, "Pass it on!" And the Chicago Corps grew.

There were younger children in the Corps who also showed talent in music. John began at first to work with them individually. Each week he visited the pawn shop with borrowed money and bought a new instrument for one of the children. The parents paid him back, a nickel or a dime a week, until his own debt was paid. Soon he had enough young people for a small band, and one of the local radio stations broadcast their music for fifteen minutes each week.

He found he was learning more and more about music by teaching. It wasn't long before he was able to buy a tuba for himself, and soon he was invited to play in the Corps' staff band. It was a great honor for a boy of sixteen, because only the finest musicians qualified for membership.

I wonder if he ever dreamed that one day he would return to be the honored guest speaker at the World Conference of Salvation Army Youth. Could he have once imagined himself on the podium before thousands of young people, invited as a living example to them, saying, "You're here because you've found the joy of knowing the Master. You're here in the very place that the Master first put me to work serving people. You've made your decision to begin a new life by placing yourself in the Master's hands, dedicating yourself to the service of Him through the service of people. Anybody here sorry about that decision?"

It was 1953. A roar of voices in unison made a joyful noise that rose, hovering over the city of Chicago. And its impact would be felt throughout the world, as each of the thousands of young people in attendance returned to their homes with new motivation to "pass it on" in service to the Master by serving His people.

CHAPTER 2

ohn felt certain that God had something special in mind for him when He gave him his particular talent. There was surely a reason that he was being led to become an artist, and specifically a potter. What John did not yet understand was how being a potter could possibly lead him to serve in the way he had promised. But his prayer was that he be led, his promise was to obey, and his faith led him forward.

It was in the fall of 1924 that John gathered all his artwork and presented himself to the Chicago Art Institute for admittance. There was no money for tuition, but he offered to work at any job they would give him for the opportunity to study at the revered Institute. He begged to be admitted.

Upon examination of the few ceramic pieces and other art he had to present, the Admissions Board agreed that he showed a certain amount

John Frank. Chicago, c. 1924.

of promise and, in consideration of his unusual determination, his application was accepted.

He packed his clothing and what little he owned in a cardboard box and rented a small room near the school.

From 5:30 to 7:30 each morning he turned eggs and hotcakes at a neighborhood grill, and they gave him breakfast. At night he guarded the famous Wedgwood Pottery collection in the museum on the fifth floor of the Institute. He swept and cleaned classrooms, prepared clays and ground glazes. He soon became the assistant to Professor Myrtle French, Head of the Ceramics Department, and stayed late to fire the kilns that finished the students' work. During the summers he worked at everything he could get hired to do in order to save enough to continue his schooling at the Institute. He was a fry cook, hauled boxes, ran errands, delivered packages, and painted signs. Other than basic living expenses, everything earned was saved for the next school term.

Professor French recognized his exceptional talent and appreciated his ambition to learn his craft at all costs. So John was given extra instruction in clays and glazes and his technical knowledge grew rapidly, along with his ability in design.

John's physique was not well developed. He had never known proper nutrition. And now, even when he could eat, he did not always take the time. As a result, he did not easily withstand the bitter Chicago winters, and frequent colds and flu robbed him of his stamina.

He enjoyed no social life whatsoever, other than church on Sunday mornings. His teachers and fellow students were virtually his only acquaintances, as he had little time to develop close relationships.

If he had a best friend, it was a young girl in his drawing class. Jenny was unusually tall and very, very thin; at best she was plain, but

"Gather ye rosebuds while ye may, old time is still a-flying." 1927. Vase created as a combination lettering and pottery project at the Chicago Art Institute.

bright and witty. A wealthy aunt was paying for her education. Although she could have attended any school she wished, she chose the Institute because she rather enjoyed art and fancied she was as good at that as anything else, and the work was not unpleasant for her. But her approach to her studies was hardly more than lackadaisical.

Jenny enjoyed watching the fury and determination with which John dove into his work. She laughed and chided him about his awful seriousness. "If it turns out you have no talent at all, Johnny boy, you'll win the prize for best try!" John's good nature and sense of humor in return for her teasing produced a bond of friendship that was to last throughout school to graduation.

John encouraged Jenny to take her studies more seriously, to stop drifting along and appreciate the opportunity of her free schooling to develop her talent. She listened because she loved to hear him talk. But it was more of a pleasure to watch him work with the fire and ambition of a young Michelangelo than to take herself seriously.

It was over a cup of hot chocolate in the commissary one day that John confessed to his friend a secret desire to take the Charles Atlas course and build his body.

"What's stopping you, Johnny boy?" asked Jenny.

"I have every intention of doing it," he replied. Hanging his head a bit, he added, "Just as soon as I have five dollars I can live without."

Jenny laughed and tossed her head. "Is that all that's between you and the body beautiful?"

"That's easy for you to say, Jenny. You're on a free ride." He wished he hadn't said that and wanted to apologize. He hadn't meant it the way it came out.

"Well, you really surprise me, Johnny! All those things you've been telling me? About how everything comes to us when we've earned it?"

During their friendship, Jenny had watched him struggle to stay in school. She had frequently observed him in class, and sometimes she thought she even sensed an energy coming from a source outside himself, flowing through his pen and onto the paper in seemingly effortless expression of thought. Yes, that was the "gift" she wished were hers, and her aunt's money couldn't buy it for her.

Suddenly Jenny was embarrassed at what she was feeling. She jumped to her feet and forced a silly laugh as she flipped a five dollar bill onto the table in front of him.

"You'll pay me back when you sell your first big statue, Johnny boy. See you in class!" And she was quickly out of sight.

For the next several months John faithfully rose an hour early each morning to execute precisely every instruction of the course. On the cover of each lesson that arrived was a picture of the wonderful Mr. Atlas—smiling, robust, King of the World—truly an inspiration to any "98-pound weakling" who felt his courage withering.

Mr. Atlas was adamant about one point in particular. Regardless of the weather, exercises were to be done in front of an open window—and nude. Luckily, John's room had only one window, and it faced a brick wall.

So no matter how the snow piled up on an already cold radiator in his small Chicago room, the rigorous demands of Mr. Atlas were met to the letter.

By the time spring arrived, John's once frail 145-pound body had become a much firmer 165. He had weathered an entire winter without sniffles, and a healthy color replaced his sallow complexion. The new vitality and feeling of wellbeing enabled him to work more easily and with more enjoyment than he had ever known.

He was to tell the story many times thereafter of the gift of five dollars that gave him the health he would maintain until the last years of his life.

*D*uring his years at the Institute, John's education in all art forms served to expand his knowledge and broaden his imagination. Whatever class assignment he was given, in virtually all media, he worked to be the best he could be in each. And his work did not go unnoticed by the staff. His oil paintings, water colors, construction projects, jewelry and ceramics, as well as art history and other academic subjects, all received his best efforts. In June of 1927, his jewelry won the Herper's Award for Excellence in Craftsmanship. He knew that whatever he learned could be useful to him sometime in his future. But he never lost his focus and ambition. Nothing could dissuade him from his goal of becoming a potter.

Mrs. French had sensed a potential greatness in her student, and because of his insatiable appetite for learning, she had given him extra hours of her time. And throughout it all, the only way he had known to show his gratitude for the many kindnesses that spoke of her faith in him was in the quality of the pottery he produced. Beyond their teacher-student relationship, there had also evolved a warm friendship.

John's mentor was a firm believer in the adage, "The optimum learning experience is to teach." It was in his third year at the Institute that a priest asked for an instructor for a class of nuns, and John was chosen without hesitation. In addition to his school work and the duties that paid his tuition, John taught ceramics one night a week.

The nuns learned pottery making, and John learned more about love and service from the sisters. It was a profound and rewarding exchange. Thereafter they lit candles for him and faithfully remembered him in their prayers, asking that he may be a light wherever the Master should send him.

As graduation neared, Mrs. French called John into her office, as she had done so many times before.

"Sit down, John, there's something I want to ask you," she began. "We haven't talked about this before. We've been too busy.

"You've done well here at the Institute, John. You've worked like a dog, and you've excelled in almost everything. Your jewelry that won the Herper's Award was outstanding and, as you know, we'll keep it here on display for a while."

John stirred uncomfortably in his chair. He knew Mrs. French well by now, and it was unlike her to call him into her office merely to pay him a compliment.

"I'm pleased you liked it."

"John, what are you going to do when you leave here? That is, do you have a job to go to? What will you do when you graduate?"

John relaxed. "Mrs. French, the good Lord has always taken care of that for me," he smiled. "When it's time to leave, I'll know where I'm going and what I'm to do. I have every faith that the right thing will present itself to me."

Her eyes looked into his with impatience. "John, you're talking like a simple child in some land of make-believe. I'm asking if you've made any applications for a position. And you're telling me that someone is going to simply walk up and offer you a job?"

John looked at her admiringly. "Mrs. French, my association with you has been more than I ever hoped for when I came here. You've been more than kind. You've been an angel sent to guide me in my learning. But," he declared with confidence, "as far as my future is concerned, I just can't believe the Master would put me here and see me through these years of preparation if He didn't have something special in mind for me."

Mrs. French sighed, and her face told him that his explanation was much too simple for her to accept.

"You see, it was no accident that I came to the Institute. I was led here. I put myself in God's hands a long time ago and told Him I didn't want to work for anyone but Him. I told Him I'd go anywhere and do anything to prepare myself for whatever He wanted me to do and be. So when it came time to find my life's work, I knew without a doubt where I had to go—no matter what I had to do to get there." He smiled and reflected, "I'd do it all over again the same way, if that's what He wanted me to do." Standing, John reassured her, "Thank you for being concerned, but I know I'll be shown where I'm supposed to go."

"Sit down, John," the matronly woman commanded abruptly. "I haven't told you yet why I called you in."

John reseated himself and waited while she shuffled through the papers on her desk. She spotted the letter she was looking for and carefully laid it down in front of her.

"I have a letter here from a Dr. Jacobson at the University of Oklahoma," she stated matter-of-factly. "He wants someone to begin a brand new ceramic art department there. Someone, he says, who can do it all—everything." She gave him a parental smile. "There are others wanting the job who are older, more experienced, and have more letters after their names, so don't get your hopes up. But John. . ."

John closed his eyes and felt butterflies begin to dance with frenzy in the pit of his stomach as he thought, "Oklahoma! Oklahoma? Isn't that where Indians live? Good heavens, will it be safe there??"

"You've been the most promising student I've ever had. And," she added facetiously, "if God wants you to go to Oklahoma, then I suppose no matter how great the competition, somehow you'll get the job. You *are interested,* aren't you?"

John rose nervously and leaned on the back of the chair.

"I'm going to recommend you highly, John. It will be a challenge for you, but I think you're well prepared for it." She nodded with an understanding smile. "I guess God has seen to that all right."

"Mrs. French, I don't know how to . . ."

"You haven't got the job yet, young man, so don't get your hopes too high. Now run along while I think about what I can say about you."

"Thank you, Mrs. French," he said respectfully, closing the door behind him.

He felt like walking.

"Oklahoma!" he pondered. "What's in Oklahoma? Well, at least they have a university. But why am I so concerned? After all, it's only an application. And besides, what are the chances they'll want me anyway? Well, if I do go, it'll certainly be an adventure."

An hour later he walked into his room. He lay on the bed and closed his eyes.

"Master, I don't know why You'd want me to go there, but then I can't see as far ahead as You can. So if that's where You want me, You know I'll go."

As he was going to sleep, he wondered how much the train fare to Oklahoma could possibly be. Trains do go to Oklahoma, don't they? He'd go by the depot on Sunday afternoon and inquire.

John Frank (left) and friend at the south side fountain of the Chicago Art Institute. 1926.

*G*raduation came and went. There had been no word from the mysterious Dr. Jacobson in Oklahoma, and that was that.

John and his friend Ralph got a job painting a large billboard on a highway near the edge of the city. The sign was in a field of tall weeds and brush. Being city boys, the perils of nature were unfamiliar to either of them.

At sundown the first day of work, they gathered their paint cans and brushes and started back to town in Ralph's old car.

It wasn't long before John began to scratch his arms and his ankles. Then Ralph began to squirm uncomfortably. By the time they arrived at John's place, little red welts had begun to appear on both their faces.

The following morning, both lay naked on the floor bathing each other in cold rags to ease the misery of what was diagnosed by a neighbor as old-fashioned poison ivy.

The kindly neighbor also brought him a letter that had been delivered that afternoon while he was away. It was from Mrs. French at the Institute. "Congratulations," it read. "You're going to Oklahoma. Drop by my office for details."

John moaned. He was puffed up like a balloon, and it was painful to move. He and Ralph began to laugh. He couldn't crawl to the door, and God was sending him to Oklahoma.

*M*ore than a week later, John walked past the familiar big stone lions that guarded the portals of the great Chicago Art Institute. Summer classes were in session. He walked up the broad stairs to the second floor, and it was like coming home.

"Johnny! Hey Johnny boy!" a voice called. And Jenny ran gleefully to meet him.

"What are you doing here, Jenny?" he laughed in surprise. "I never expected to see you again!"

"I just came back to pick up a few things. I'm so glad to see you! Tell me—are you rich and famous yet?" Together they laughed and began walking arm in arm down the long corridor.

"Tell me what you're up to, Johnny!" she urged.

"You know that job at the University of Oklahoma I told you about? Well, it seems they want me! I'm going to see Mrs. French right now to find out about it."

"Oh, that's wonderful! When are you going?"

"I don't know. And I also don't know how I'm going to get there," he confessed. "It'll take fifty dollars just for the fare!"

"There you go again, Johnny. Is fifty dollars all that's standing between you and the great opportunity?" she scolded.

John didn't answer but walked straight ahead. "Jenny, you're out of my league. You just don't understand. Getting to the job will take as much as I can make in a month—and that's if I don't eat." He turned to face her. "You just don't understand what money is all about."

"Oh yes, I do," she replied soberly. "I know it's terribly important when you don't have it. But when you have lots of it, it's not important at all, except for the pleasure of watching it work doing things it's meant to do."

John searched her face. Why had he never noticed how beautiful she really was? Had God pulled those mysterious strings once again? Was it really coincidence that their paths had crossed again, today of all days?

Jenny fumbled in her purse for a pen. "Please, Johnny!" she begged. "Don't pass up this opportunity for the lack of a silly fifty dollars!"

She scrawled her name at the bottom of a check and handed it to him. "You know I'll not miss it," she beamed. "Now you won't worry about getting there. Your path is clear. Fame and glory await you! So get going!"

John stood looking at her, unable to say all that he was feeling. Jenny had once before given him a gift that started him on the road to the health he now enjoyed. Now she was filling another important need—a ticket to his first professional job.

"God bless you, Jenny. You're truly an angel. You know I'll never be able to repay you," he stammered.

"You don't understand, Johnny. You see, this is my poor payment in return for what you've given me." She kissed his cheek. "Now go out there and show those Oklahomans what you're made of. I'm expecting great things of you, Johnny boy!"

"Goodbye, Jenny," he said, as he affectionately embraced her. "God will surely go with you."

"I don't know. Sometimes I think He doesn't know I'm alive," she said a bit sadly. "But," she added brightly, "if He really does exist, you've sure got Him on your side. Good luck, Johnny!"

John watched her turn away and hurry down the corridor, and he knew he would never see her again. But he would never forget the significant role she had played in his life.

God does surely work in strange and mysterious ways.

CHAPTER 3

John arrived in Norman, Oklahoma, early in August, 1927, with one suitcase and great expectations. After a warm welcome from Dr. Jacobson, they chatted and walked toward the armory building. The door was open, and they proceeded to a dark space at the rear.

"Here we are, John," he announced. "It's all yours."

John looked around the room bewildered. It had obviously been empty and unused for some time, except by assorted rodents, critters, and creatures that crawled. Cautiously making his way through cobwebs and debris, he tried to make it match in any respect what he had envisioned prior to his arrival. It was no use.

Dusting himself off, he returned to the doorway where Dr. Jacobson stood studying the young man's face for a reaction.

"What do you think, John?"

"Looks like I'd better get to work right away, sir!" John forced cheerfully. "When do I start?"

Satisfied with the response, Dr. Jacobson replied, "You'll want to get settled first. Do you have a place to live?"

"No, I just got off the train an hour ago. Where do you suggest I look?"

"The administration building is right down this street. The bulletin board usually carries a listing of what's available near the campus."

They shook hands, and John thanked him kindly.

"Good luck, John. Drop by my office in the morning, and we'll get started. Glad to have you with us."

On his way to the administration building, John stopped to listen to a loud, strange, rasping noise coming from the trees. He stopped a student who was walking toward him.

"Excuse me. Can you tell me what's making that strange sound?"

"Oh, that? Ha! Those are katydids."

"Katydids?"

"You must be new here," he said, noticing John's suitcase.

"I just arrived from Chicago this morning. Are they always around?"

"The katydids? Only in summer. The hotter it gets, the louder they sing. You'll get used to them."

John thanked the young man and continued his walk. He was accustomed to heat, but the air in Oklahoma was oppressively heavy and humid. "So this is Oklahoma in summer!" he thought, wiping the perspiration from his face. "Whew!"

Inside the door of the red brick building he spotted a bulletin board. Only two slips of paper were pinned to it, and one said, "Gentlemen Only, Room and Board, $25 per month."

After getting directions from the girl at the desk, he began to walk south and away from the campus.

"Well, Lord," he said under his breath, "here I am. I'll do my best."

The rooming house was pleasant enough, and the meals would be regular. At supper that evening he became acquainted with the other boarders with whom he would be sharing meals. Unlike the people from where he had come, they were friendly, relaxed, and unhurried.

Everyone sat on the front porch after the sun had set and lazily fanned themselves. John sat on the step and asked questions about the weather, the people, the university, and katydids.

After sleeping sitting up in a train for two nights, his new bed was a welcome sight. He lay awake and thought about his first day.

There were thoughts of the gentle-mannered Dr. Jacobson and the comfortable rapport he felt when they met. He would very much enjoy working for him, and he resolved to prove himself in no time at all.

Then the image of his new classroom returned.

"That room is sure baffling, Master. Oh, cleaning it up won't be hard. But it's empty! I have no equipment, no tools, no kiln . . . there's not even a light bulb!"

He turned over and closed his eyes.

"Well, you didn't promise me it would be easy. But stick with me, and I know I can do it. You'll see."

A week passed. John had enthusiastically cleaned and thoroughly washed down the walls and floor of the room in which he was to teach his first class.

"Dr. Jacobson, when can I get a kiln? And I need some clay tools. I'll have to order some materials. Where will my supplies come from? The students need benches and tables to work on, and a potter's wheel, and, and . . ."

The distinguished gentleman behind the heavy oak desk held up his hand to signal a halt.

"Easy, John. First things first. It'll all come in time," he calmy assured the anxious new teacher. "Let me remind you that this is a brand new department. Rome wasn't built in a day either."

"Without being disrespectful, sir, what exactly is available to me? Classes will begin in a little more than three weeks, and I'd like to be prepared."

Taking him to the window, the tall scholarly gentleman pointed to a nearby building.

"Tell maintenance I sent you. You should find plenty of lumber there and some nails and a hammer. And don't forget to look around for some electrical cord and sockets. You can't work in the dark, you know."

John stared blankly at Dr. Jacobson for a moment, then smiled knowingly. "Now I understand what Mrs. French meant by 'someone who can do everything.'"

"Precisely," he smiled with a nod. "That's why we hired you and not the others. We were told you could build, do electrical work, follow orders cheerfully, and weren't afraid of hard work. Oh yes," he added as if it were an afterthought, "she also said you would be an excellent ceramics teacher."

Now that the two men understood each other perfectly, they shook hands and began to laugh.

"Dr. Jacobson, if you'll excuse me, I've got work to do," said John. "I'll see you in a few days!"

He closed the door behind him and chuckled to himself as he broke into a spirited gait across the campus lawn.

"Okay, Master, now I hear You! Every time I start feeling a little too important, You bring me right back to reality. But I do thank You, 'cause now I know what I'm supposed to do!"

*T*he following Sunday morning John introduced himself to the Reverend Milton Smith at the Church of the Nazarene.

Reverend Smith was a recent seminary graduate, and the Norman church was his very first post. The two men had this in common, and John felt a great affinity for him and his young wife Opal. He was often invited to their home for Sunday dinners.

John easily made friends in the church and on campus. Soon he was feeling very much at home in the community.

*J*ohn was ready when the fall semester began. There were several tables and benches at which his students would work. There was a handmade clay storage box partly full, two potter's wheels, a few tools—and lights! But no kiln.

About a dozen students enrolled in the University of Oklahoma's first ceramics class. But it was near Thanksgiving before a small kiln arrived in which to fire the students' work. John was excited and proud of his new toy, the final item that completed his new department.

John was a natural teacher. He encouraged creative freedom and maintained the idea that it should be fun, not work. Although several of his students were his own age, they respected him as if he were a full professor.

OU Tepee. Logo used from 1928-1933 to mark pottery made at the University of Oklahoma Ceramic Art Department.

Word of the class spread quickly. By the second semester, he had built more tables and benches. The class was limited to twenty students, and rather than turn anyone away, he added another class. He was fast becoming a popular instructor on the campus.

The State of Oklahoma was given funds by the Federal government to conduct a geological survey. At that time, there was little to attract people to Oklahoma to live and work. The nation as a whole was in a depression. And with most farms in Oklahoma having been wiped out with the dust bowl, people were leaving to find work elsewhere because there were virtually no jobs and little to stay for.

The idea of the survey was that if Oklahoma's many clay deposits could be mapped, then analyzed to determine the best use for each, the state could conceivably become a major center for industrial ceramics, thus providing more jobs. After all, there were thousands of products made of "baked earth," a material used more than any other to make everything from light sockets to spark plugs to bricks and automobile and aircraft parts.

Oklahoma was a good candidate for the manufacture of all kinds of ceramics, for more reasons than just its abundance of clay. The price of a thousand cubic feet of natural gas in Oklahoma could be used for no more than a few cents, compared to, say, Chicago, where prices could be as costly as $1.40 to fire a kiln. In some states, prices might rise to an outrageous two dollars or more. Multiple firings each week on a continuing basis certainly made the tremendous cost difference in gas alone a plus for Oklahoma.

The director of the geological survey hired John during his first year at OU to travel the state looking for clay deposits that would be suitable for pottery on a commercial level. In addition, wide advertising encouraged people with clay on their land to submit samples to him for free analysis.

That year John collected over a hundred samples from all over Oklahoma, but most of them contained too much silica (sand). They were not cost effective, because they required extensive processing to refine, and many needed too many expensive additives to provide the ingredients they lacked.

One clay did stand out from all the others, however, and it was one found about seven miles southeast of the town of Ada in the southern part of the state. The deposit was about twenty feet thick and covered several acres. It yielded readily to preparation and fired successfully at 1950-2000° F . It was plastic, porous, dried well without warping or cracking, and fired beautifully.

To John, the find was the end of the rainbow! The Ada clay had all he was looking for and more. It had a good body, good color, and it fired at the temperature he needed in order to produce a strong and durable product. It bonded well with the glazes he was then using and with others he wanted to experiment with. In the meantime, there was no reason his students shouldn't enjoy the advantages of working with this excellent clay. So he immediately replaced the commercial clay bought for his classes with the new-found Ada clay.

As early as this, John's mind was working on developing a one-fire process. And this Ada clay, he suspected, would be the one he could eventually use for that ambitious purpose. Few ceramicists, if any, have ever perfected the one-fire. Normally, a piece is fired without glaze, then glazed and fired a second time. However, if the glaze could be applied to the raw clay and fired only once, the cost of producing it would drop dramatically in fuel alone, along with handling and overall manufacturing and labor costs.

But in order to be successful with a one-fire, many factors would have to be adjusted and coordinated. There was of course the temperature,

John Frank (right) with the first load of Ada clay.
Ada, Oklahoma, c. November, 1927.

both warming and cooling times, and the length of fire at peak
temperature. Then, too, the only glazes available at that time were
designed for the two-fire process. Glazes that could meet all these same
rigorous demands, working with the clay at the same times and
temperatures, would have to be developed from scratch because they
simply had not yet been invented. The only glazes available were those
designed for the two-fire process.

It was a colossal challenge. Because nobody believed it could be
done, he would receive little encouragement or help to achieve the
desired end result.

But he had faith that one day he would hit upon the right formulas
and combinations that would allow clay and glaze to synchronize in
only one firing and emerge as something attractive that people would
want to buy and live with. Although there was never a mention of it to
anyone, he was all the while looking ahead and envisioning a time that
he would own his own pottery manufacturing business. All that he was
doing at the University was just grist for the mill.

Before Christmas, John bought his first car and learned to
drive. It was a used Model-T Ford, and it set him back
seventy-five dollars.

At church one Sunday in January, John was introduced to a student named Fred Bowman, a tall, lanky boy from western Oklahoma whose father was a Nazarene minister. The two shared many interests, and they soon began to go places together.

"Want to go to church in Bethany on Sunday, John? It's right on the Bethany College campus, and we can probably meet some pretty girls."

John had been so busy at school, he hadn't taken the time to think about girls. It sounded okay to him.

"Sure, why not? I need a day away from here."

"If we don't find anything we like there," suggested Fred, "we could call my sister in Oklahoma City. She has a new roommate I haven't met, and we could all go for a ride."

Bethany was just west of Oklahoma City, almost a two-hour drive from Norman. So the boys got up earlier than usual on Sunday morning and cranked up John's Model-T. It ran like a top! They laughed and talked all the way about all the girls there would be to choose from.

When they were seated in church, John looked around to find it half empty, and not one pretty coed in sight. What a let down! He looked at Fred sternly for an explanation.

"I forgot," whispered Fred. "It's between semesters, and they've all gone home. Sorry. But don't worry—we'll find something."

After the two had had a pleasant Sunday dinner in the home of Fred's friends, he called his sister in the city.

"I've got someone I want you to meet, Sis," he shouted into the receiver. "We're over here in Bethany. What are you and your roommate doing this afternoon?"

After a pause, "What? Oh, he's a teacher. Could we come and take you girls for a drive this afternoon?" A longer pause. "I know the other one was a bore, but this one's different. Don't you want to meet him? What else have you got to do today?"

Fred strained to hear the voice at the other end. "All right, Sis," he beamed. "We're leaving right now. See you in a while!"

He hurried to the car where John was waiting.

"It's all set. You'll like my sister. She's kinda tall and slim and blonde. . ."

"Sure, Fred, I'll like her. Anyway, what else have we got to do?"

"*S*is, this is John Frank. John, this is my sister, Grace Lee," said Fred grandly.

"Hello," replied Grace Lee charmingly. "Fred, this is my roommate, Mona."

Fred nodded and forced a smile. Oh well, they had nothing else to do today. The girls took turns sitting on Fred's lap while John drove. A Model-T easily sat two, but four was a squeeze.

When your best friend wants to introduce you to his sister, you can't expect a lot. But Grace Lee was a pleasant surprise. She had pretty blonde hair, a slender shapely figure, a charming smile, and just a touch of shyness.

Soon Fred was driving the car, and the girls were taking turns sitting on John's lap. Now John was free to exchange glances and smiles with Grace Lee.

Late in the afternoon the four sat on the porch of the girls' rooming house as the boys prepared to drive back to Norman.

"May I call you sometime?" asked John. "I'd like to see you again, if it's all right with you."

"My phone number is Maple 724. You'd better write it down," she said.

"Maple 724. I can remember that."

"Are you sure? I can write it down for you."

"I'll remember," he assured her. "Would you like to go out Friday night?"

Grace Lee coyly shrugged a shoulder. "All right. What time?"

John squeezed her hand. "I'll pick you up at eight o'clock sharp!"

On the way home, he thanked Fred for the birthday present.

"This is your birthday?"

"No, tomorrow, the 31st. You're right. Grace Lee is pretty, isn't she?"

*M*onday's students noticed that a change had come over Mr. Frank since last Friday. His face was a bit flushed, they thought. And although they were accustomed to seeing him smile a lot, they observed that today he could not stop smiling, and he moved about with unusually quick energy.

"Mr. Frank must be in love," someone commented out loud.

"Looks to me like he's glowing pink," said another.

"What's the matter, Mr. Frank?" a voice chimed from the back of the room, "the love bug bite you on the weekend?"

Everyone had a good laugh. John blushed and laughed with them.

"Now let's settle down, class, and get to work," he said, but still with good humor.

He turned away quickly and continued to busy himself.

"Is it showing that much?" he wondered to himself. "Good heavens! Could I really be in love?"

John did not wish to appear too anxious, so he waited until Tuesday to give Grace Lee a call.

"Elm 724 in Oklahoma City please, operator," he said brightly.

"Hello? This is the Rexall Pharmacy."

Slowly John placed the receiver back on the hook. Picking it up again, he told the operator, "Ma'am, I'm calling Elm 724 in Oklahoma City, and you just gave me a wrong number. Would you please try again?"

"Hello? This is the Rexall Pharmacy."

"Is this Elm 724?"

"Sure is, what can I do for you?"

"Nothing. I've changed my mind."

John sat bewildered. "Is she playing games with me? Did she give me the wrong number by mistake? Surely a girl ought to know her own phone number. Maybe she did that to brush me off."

As far as he knew, he still had a date with Grace Lee on Friday, although now he considered not going. Much better that *he* stand *her* up than to drive all the way to the city to find she's out with someone else.

It was a depressing week, and he felt very foolish at having fallen so hard in one afternoon's meeting. He was deeply hurt and part of him wanted to erase the whole incident from his mind.

In the meantime, Grace Lee waited in her room each night, hoping

John would call. "I know he's a very busy man, Mona, but he did ask for my number. Do you think he'll be here on Friday?"

The week at last dragged to an end. John pressed his only suit and donned his new blue tie. If she was there, he was determined to make the best possible impression. If she wasn't, he had certainly learned his lesson.

John's stomach was uneasy all the way to the city. The closer he got to her rooming house, the more he thought of turning back. Nevertheless, he wanted once and for all to know the truth and resolved to go through with it, painful or not.

At ten minutes before eight o'clock, he strode up the front steps and knocked loudly. Immediately the door swung open, and there stood Grace Lee, smiling radiantly, looking lovely in a pale blue dress.

John stood frozen. There she was! She was really there!

"Don't stand out there in the cold, John," chirped Grace Lee. "Come on in!" She took his hand and led him into the parlor. "Let me take your coat."

John sank into the nearest chair.

"What's the matter?" she asked. "Cat got your tongue?"

"You look absolutely beautiful! Uh—that is—I didn't expect to see you . . ."

"We have a date tonight, haven't we? I thought you'd call me this week."

"I did, but you gave me the wrong number."

"Wrong number?"

"I kept getting a drug store."

"What number did you call?"

"I called the number you gave me—Elm 724. And it was a drug store!"

"I told you to write it down," she laughed. "I said Maple 724, not Elm."

"Oh," he moaned in embarrassment. "I'm sorry. Can you forgive me? I actually thought that you'd . . . oh, never mind, let's go to dinner and forget it."

But Grace Lee was never to let him forget how close they came to never knowing each other beyond one afternoon in a crowded Model-T.

John took Grace Lee to church the following Sunday morning, and in the afternoon there was a band concert in the park. They held hands all day, and laughed and strolled and talked.

The sun set much too soon, and it was painful for John to think of leaving her. There was only one thing to do.

"Grace Lee, will you marry me?"

"I don't know, John. I met you only a week ago."

"Say yes . . ."

"I won't say no . . ."

"That's good enough! Can I see you again next Friday night?"

The day before, John had made a lovely vase on the potter's wheel with her in mind. It was ten inches high, full and round at

**A present for Grace Lee.
February, 1928.**

the bottom, then tapered gracefully into a long slender neck not unlike a bud vase, with a small fluted lip at the top. He wrote both their names on the bottom, with two arrows pointing from his name to hers. He would finish it that week with a mirrored black glaze, fire it and present it to her the next weekend as a token of his love. For now, it was all he had to give her.

John was not yet earning a large enough salary to properly court a lady. But it didn't seem to matter to either of them. So the courtship took place for the most part on a tennis court in a park near Grace Lee's rooming house.

Although Fred liked John a lot, he didn't know him well enough. It quite unnerved him that his sister had suddenly become so dizzy about a man she knew so little about.

"Do you realize what you're doing, Sis? You don't even know his family. What kind of a person is he? You could be hurt very badly, you know!"

"But he's such a wonderful man, Fred . . . kind, affectionate, talented, ambitious . . ."

"How do you know you love him?"

"Did I say I loved him?"

"Aw, Sis, it's written all over you. You've both got stars in your eyes!"

"Oh, really?" she giggled. "Then I—I guess we're in love."

Fred shook his head gravely and went to find John.

"I need a place to live till the semester is over, John," lied Fred. "Suppose I could move in with you for a while?"

"Sure, Fred, if you really need to. But you know how small the room is."

"That's all right. In a while we'll find a larger one closer to campus."

Fred found a phone and called Grace Lee.

"It's okay, Sis, I'm moving in with John next week. Don't worry about a thing. I'll be close enough to check him out close up."

"But, Fred! Do you really think that's necessary? It just seems so . . . so dishonest!"

"You can't be too careful, Sis. You just can't be too careful!"

Spring arrived. Fred had carefully observed at close range the character and daily habits of his new roommate. But he found John Frank to be virtuous in all ways. His love for Grace Lee had inspired his work to new heights, and they had only become more and more devoted to each other.

"Okay, Sis," Fred conceded. "I won't mention it ever again. He's all yours."

Wedding portrait. Norman, Oklahoma, September 4, 1928.

*J*ohn and Grace Lee set their wedding date for Christmas of that
year. Then it was for Thanksgiving. But on September 4th,
1928, Grace Lee's twenty-third birthday, they found themselves
standing in the minister's living room saying, "Until death do us part."

The couple looked forward to a weekend honeymoon at their new
modest home, a small converted garage apartment on Lahoma Street.
Alone at last.

But not for long. John's youngest brother Francis arrived from
Chicago that afternoon to enroll at the university and promptly moved
into the little house with them. At best, the space was cramped for

two, but seemed even smaller when Francis came tramping through the newlyweds' miniature bedroom on late night trips to the bathroom.

It seemed at once apparent to Grace Lee that she had married not one, but two men.

John's salary was a meager $177.77 per month, and he had waited until after the wedding to confess to his new bride that he had previously incurred a personal debt of one hundred dollars. It was a shocking, astronomical sum to Grace Lee, and she resolved to go to work and pay it off as quickly as possible.

She carried an excellent letter of reference from the job she had left in Oklahoma City. But now she was a faculty wife. To be an office worker was unthinkable. It just wasn't done.

Her only alternative was to enroll at the University and earn the hours necessary for a teaching credential. Tuition being free to faculty and wives, it allowed her to also study voice and piano, an ambition heretofore unaffordable.

It soon became evident that three could not live as cheaply as two, but they would manage somehow. John gathered some scrap lumber and added a small sleeping porch onto the rear of the house for Francis.

They celebrated their first wedding anniversary, and Grace Lee began teaching school in a neighboring town. Her salary that year paid the one hundred dollar debt and left just enough extra to help buy a better car.

In the meantime, the Franks began socializing with other young couples on the university faculty, as well as with Opal and Milton Smith and their friends at the church.

Many couples their own age had already begun families, and those who hadn't were making plans. After three long winters had passed, John and Grace Lee were still talking of having a child.

"We can't possibly afford it, John, if I quit work," she often fretted. "And I can't teach while I'm . . . you know."

"But we should have children while we're young, honey! You know we'll get along somehow."

By the time winter had turned to spring and spring to summer, Grace Lee, along with all else in nature, gave way to her nesting instincts, and I was summoned.

CHAPTER 4

The Franks. Norman, Oklahoma, 1932. John and Grace Lee pose with Donna outside the house on Lahoma Street.

I was born in the spring of 1932 with a good and healthy start. But at nine months, a small red spot appeared on the side of my face and began growing at an alarming rate. The doctors diagnosed it as a rare type of cancerous growth and urged that I be taken at once to the Mayo Clinic.

The only treatment known at the time for that which threatened my life required the use of radium, and there were no guarantees that it would be successful. The risks were high. If it did not work, I would most likely die; if it did work, I would surely be left with massive facial scars, and possibly mental impairment, results not uncommon with the application of radium to the head and face. Their parental ambitions for me were much the same as those of all parents, and naturally they were stricken with dreadful fears that I would go through life disfigured. They had a hard choice to make, and they had to make it quickly. The risk had to be taken.

Fortunately for us, the famous clinic in Rochester, Minnesota, charged for services according to the family's ability to pay. When our financial status was learned, efforts to save my life were offered at a nominal fee, the payments to be spread over a period of several years. In addition, the clinic provided train fare for our many visits during the following twelve months.

Because of my age, the specialists there wisely administered many more treatments than normal, and in much smaller doses. In this way, I was eventually freed of all evidence that the growth had ever existed, with no adverse physical or mental side effects.

By late summer of 1933, the fear of losing me had passed. My treatments were about to conclude; only two more trips to Rochester were scheduled. Some semblance of normality would soon be returning to our lives, and Daddy's ambition was urging him to enter the business world. Mother wanted him to wait another year, as she feared the loss of a regular income, but she could not deny his drive and his determination.

"God is pointing me in that direction, honey. I've got no choice!" insisted my dreamer father.

"Well, I guess if we fail, we're still young enough to begin again," conceded my practical mother.

It soon became imperative that we move to larger quarters. When a "For Sale" sign appeared on the house on the lot in front of ours, Daddy decided we could do worse for the money. The payments would be thirty-two dollars each month, and Mother fretted that it was an obligation we might not be able to meet. But Daddy believed the money would come, and we moved anyway.

Starting a new business in a depression was of course madness, but Daddy was optimistic and cheerfully set about looking for a place that he could convert to a studio to begin making his pottery.

We had barely moved into our new house when Grandpa Frank arrived from Chicago, leaving Grandma in the city that she refused to leave for anyone or anything. Recently retired from the telephone company, he was eager to come and help Daddy get his business started.

To find a building in Daddy's financial range was not an easy task. It was not even a whole building that he bought. It had been partly burned, and much work was needed to as much as keep out the rain.

The charred lumber was torn down, but it was not wasted. Soon we had a new living room on the front of our house.

In addition to his teaching, Daddy began making pottery nights and weekends, with Mother's help. It was a long shot, but in August of 1934 he took some of his pottery to the Chicago Gift and Art Show in hopes of getting some orders. At the end of the first day, he wrote us a letter. "Honies—" it said, "I've had a busy day. I've written $35 worth of orders! That's pretty good. I'm tired, and I have to write up my orders. I miss you, your Honey."

Soon after Daddy came home, a young man knocked at our door and introduced himself as Andrew Lester. He had heard of my father and came to the university to study ceramics.

Andy had no job, no place to live, and no money for tuition. But my father, remembering how he had arrived at the Chicago Art Institute with little more than his ambition to be an artist, set about helping the boy find a job. He remembered how he had been so generously helped, and this was his chance to "pass it on" to another young artist-to-be.

In addition to milking cows and cleaning stables at the local dairy, Andy mowed our yard, cleaned our house, cooked breakfast, washed dishes, and often took care of me in exchange for room and board.

Andy was a born artist. At twelve years old he had sculpted a remarkable life-sized bust of his fourth-great-grandfather, Davy Crockett, which was on display at the Alamo in San Antonio, Texas. With my parents' generosity and encouragement, our young boarder went on to become a leading Americana sculptor. In 1968 he created a second bust of Crockett which stands alongside the first at that shrine. Today scores of sculptures and busts representing many famous American heros grace capitol buildings, schools and universities, museums, and private collections throughout the nation, all bearing the signature of Andrew Lester.

There were six of us in the house now. Grandpa, Uncle Francis, and Andy slept on cots on the sleeping porch. My crib was next to Mother and Daddy's bed in the little bedroom.

Because most of the floor and some of the walls in our new living room were made of charred wood, black footprints and the smell of charcoal filled the house. Mother and Andy worked in vain to keep it looking clean.

As for me, I skipped the normal crawling stage. I found it made far better sense to keep my eyes straight ahead and look where I was going while I sat upright and scooted on my seat. Mother was dismayed when my black-bottomed diapers quickly became tattered rags and had to be replaced much too frequently.

These were hard times indeed, but if my mother and father were anything, they were resourceful. Grandpa and Grandma Bowman raised chickens and rabbits, and the feed they bought for their animals came in sacks made of one yard of pretty cotton print material. Each sack was washed and sent to us for Mother to sew dresses for me. Although we lived without many of the things we now call necessities, I was always dressed in very pretty clothes.

$\mathcal{T}$hrough the efforts of our entire household, a reasonable facsimile of a small pottery factory came into being during that scorching summer of record-high temperatures.

Daddy continued to teach at the university and work nights and weekends making his own pottery. Mother washed and ironed clothes for four men, cared for me, worked in the new office (a desk), and managed to cook meals for us all as well. When an occasional customer came to look at Daddy's pottery, she was hostess and saleslady. The wares were displayed on three wooden shelves above the casting bench.

Four students were soon hired to help build up a stock of pottery. But more often than not there was no money to pay them, so Daddy invited them to have lunch and supper at our house. Mother found scores of ways to fix hamburger meat, as the price was only three pounds for twenty-five cents. Often there was only day-old bread and meat loaf to eat. However, it was a better meal than most of them would have otherwise had, and they happily accepted it in lieu of money.

My father's fledgling company operated under the name, "Frank Potteries" from summer 1933 through February, 1934. It was then that Mother suggested that a change of name might give the product a more salable image. Being the only commercial pottery in the state, my parents borrowed the last three letters of Oklahoma and came up with "Frankoma." It had a successful ring to it! And spirits were lifted to see FRANKOMA POTTERIES on the new sign painted above the door of the little factory.

*I*n the meantime, Daddy was still a member of the university staff and, as such, he had certain social obligations to meet.

When my mother needed a dress to wear, her friend Mabel came to help her dye the one she had worn before, in hopes no one would recognize it. Or sometimes Mother found a remnant and made a new skirt. Once she and Mabel sewed a beautiful lace dress from one of our curtains to attend an important reception at the home of the university president. No matter what her clothes were made from, Mother held her head high and wore them as if they had come from the most expensive store in town. And no one ever thought they had not.

Close friends often gathered at our house for parties. Because times were lean for everyone, none had much more to offer than we did. But the parties were great fun, and they served as a relief from the struggles for survival in a depression.

Although we were short of chairs, no one minded sitting on the floor. Mabel and Aubrey, Paul and Irene, Joe and Elsie, and Opal and Milton were our most frequent visitors. Almost everyone had small children, and they were all called upon at various times to be my baby sitters.

Even though Joe and Elsie Taylor had no children, I liked to go to their house most of all, because they had a wonderful big cat they had gotten from South America and had raised from a baby. They called it an ocelot, and his name was Teeger, but I think they spelled it "Tigre," his name in Columbia where he was born.

I could tell it made Mother kind of nervous for me to be there. But Joe and Elsie were always duly cautious, because they said Tigre was a wild animal, and wild animals could sometimes be "unpredictable." I was never afraid of Tigre, because we liked each other a lot, and I knew he would never hurt me. Joe taught sculpture at the University, and he used Tigre as a model for many of his cat sculptures. He was the cat that was used in Frankoma's first trademark, the pot and puma, symbolizing both sculpture and fine artware. The friendship between Daddy and Joe would continue long past those days in Norman, and Daddy would go on producing in pottery many of the sculptures that Joe created. Joe's first baby head sculpture was of me when I was nine months old. Thereafter, he received many commissions to do children's heads and became well known for them. But mine was his first.

y father submitted his letter of resignation to the university early in 1936 and finished the spring semester. Frankoma Potteries looked remarkably profitable on paper. So many pieces would be made, they would sell them for certain prices, and the profit would be a swell figure over in the far column.

However, there was no money to advertise, and the factory was far from any possible walk-in trade. The only way the pottery could be sold was to load it into our old sedan and peddle it to businesses around Norman for resale. The drug stores, gift shops,

Donna Frank, nine months, 1932. The first baby head sculpture created by Joe Taylor.

and hardware stores hesitated to buy, not knowing what prices they could possibly bring in a depression. A few merchants reluctantly accepted one or two items on consignment. The cash was definitely not flowing.

One day a fast-talking salesman called on Daddy. He said he was very impressed with the style of the product and offered to take almost all of the existing stock to sell. But rather than sending the man out to represent Frankoma Potteries in the dirty, broken down old car he was driving, Daddy generously offered to trade cars with him for a few days. The man drove away in a cloud of dust, and we never saw him again.

hen a man named Frank Ellis came to our town, praising and flattering his way into Daddy's confidence, begging permission to sell stock in the wonderful new Frankoma Potteries. The money would enable Daddy and Mother to expand the business, buy some needed equipment and supplies, and perhaps begin to pay salaries to their hardworking people. It was a way for Frankoma to get on its feet and move ahead.

Pot & Puma. Early Frankoma
trademark used from 1935–1938.

Frank Ellis sold shares at one hundred dollars each, but Daddy never saw a cent of it. And what little money found its way to the cash drawer always disappeared after a visit from Mr. Ellis. "Expenses, John, expenses!" he'd laugh as he drove away in his shiny car.

Soon there was no money to fix the old car that had been left in place of the fairly decent one we'd once had. Then we hadn't enough food to feed ourselves, much less those who worked at Frankoma. We had to forfeit our house to the mortgage company because there was no money to make the payments.

Uncle Francis married and moved away. Andy was now living elsewhere. Grandpa Frank died on Christmas Day.

There seemed nowhere to turn for even a place to live. Just days before we were to be put out onto the street, Daddy became acquainted with an elderly widow who lived in a very large three-story house in Norman. She had become unable to maintain the house alone, and was persuaded by her family to move to a smaller place. She would allow us to live there in exchange for some stock in Frankoma Potteries.

We thus graduated from an unreasonably small living space to a veritable mansion. But it was by no means into luxury that we moved. We began to know how Jonah must have felt living in the belly of the giant whale.

The ceilings were ten and twelve feet high, so the rooms were impossible to heat. Mother hauled buckets of coal from the basement several times a day, where she often encountered one of the snakes that made the dark dungeon their winter home.

The old potbelly stoves deposited thick layers of black soot on the floors, walls, and furniture. Our food was cooked on a coal stove, and tasted like it. There was no getting away from it. Our clothes took on a telltale gray and smelled of musty soot. Only cold water flowed from those taps that worked at all, and food again became scarce.

I was four that spring. Although we had always faithfully gone to church, Mother and Daddy made the unhappy decision to stay home that Easter Sunday because our clothes were not good enough to wear. Mother was not feeling well enough to go anyway. Her face was growing pale, and she was becoming very ill.

On Easter morning a giant bouquet of roses arrived. Mother was undernourished and fatigued, and Frank Ellis had used money from the company till to send her flowers. It was the next to the last straw.

The camel's back was broken that very afternoon when Mrs. Ellis and her little Joanne paid a cheerful visit, both handsomely dressed in expensive new clothes. I stood in awe at the sight of Joanne. Her shiny patent leather slippers, crisp organdy dress, and flowered bonnet with ribbons made her look like the princess in my fairy tale book. When they left our house, Mother emotionally and physically collapsed.

It wasn't long before Aunt Mae, Mother's sister, came to take care of her. She and Uncle Joe and my cousin Leon moved into the rooms on the second floor. Leon became my friend, my hero, and a pleasant distraction from those awful winter months.

It was only about a year that my parents had struggled to maintain themselves in the old mansion, but it seemed an eternity. The discomforts we suffered made my parents desperate to leave the old "house of horrors" at any cost.

Soon Daddy found a little house nearby, and the rent was cheap. It was located, ironically, on Frank Street. Not much larger than the little house we had known before, Mother and Daddy laughingly called it the "cracker box." But happily there were only three of us.

The old gray mansion was sold and made into a funeral home. How appropriate it would be—to serve the dead.

T he doctors were reluctant to diagnose my mother's illness. They had hoped that the move would help her, but it did not. She seemed to retain the damp and chill of the old mansion, and their best advice was that she go away for a long rest.

So Mother and I boarded a bus for West Virginia to visit Daddy's sister Ruth, and her family. I was five years old, and children traveled free.

Before we arrived at our destination, Mother caught a dreadful cold. It took most of our visit for her to regain enough strength to travel again. Then on our way back home, she was suddenly stricken with something more than a cold. She was on the verge of collapse when we got off the bus in St. Louis.

Mother was rushed to the St. Louis Hospital where the attending doctors prepared to remove her appendix the following morning. But Mother knew she was suffering from something other than appendicitis and steadfastly refused to submit to surgery.

Nothing the doctors said could persuade her. In a few days she dressed herself and weakly led me onto a bus headed for home sweet home.

While we were away, Daddy had loaded our car Packard with his pottery and had hit the road to peddle his wares. He had some success in selling to a few stores in Oklahoma City. There was a bit of cash at last. We would need it.

*D*uring the weeks that followed, my mother's condition only continued to worsen. Several specialists were consulted to see what could be done. There was barely enough money to try one more doctor. Then one day a Dr. Gertrude Nielsen was highly recommended.

The Hungarian-born woman of uncanny intuition and skill went to work and within hours announced that, for one thing, my mother was pregnant. Pregnant?!

Eyes blinked, and my parents looked into each other's faces. Then they broke into laughter and began hugging and kissing each other.

"Strange," I thought, "how they can be so happy about my mother being so sick. And what does that word mean?"

Before I knew it, I was swept into their arms and forced to join in a happiness I didn't understand. They told me I was going to have a little brother or sister before long, and I was soberly unimpressed.

But the celebration soon ended, as that was only the good news. The bad news was that there was a complication called Malta fever (also known as undulant fever), about which very little was known at the time.

Other cases of the disease were soon discovered in the area, and the source was quickly traced to one of the local dairies. The establishment was immediately closed and the infected animals put to death.

The problem now was not only to treat the illness and save my mother, but to save the child she carried as well.

Dear Dr. Nielsen was a brilliant and dedicated woman in the field of medicine. Although my mother's condition lingered, Dr. Nielsen watched and treated her carefully over the next several months and brought her through the crisis. She worked as if we had all the money in the world, but never was there mention of a fee. She knew she would be paid some day. It wasn't important. Not one life, but two lives, depended upon her.

Mother followed Dr. Nielsen's orders to the letter and began to improve steadily. Since there was no way of knowing when the pregnancy had begun, the doctor's observations led her to guess that the date of birth would be somewhere around February 22nd.

In an effort to include me in the event, my mother called me into the bedroom one afternoon and said she had something to tell me. She began very seriously to explain to me something about a seed that Daddy had planted, but I was unable to link it in my mind with anything to do with babies and things. It was all so vague.

Later I wandered about in the yard and carefully examined the flower bed to see if any new plants had come up along the side of the house. I remember thinking that what my mother was trying to say was probably not very important anyway, or she would have been more explicit.

Leon now lived only a few blocks away, and although he was still my favorite friend, we didn't get to play together so often anymore. But I asked him one day about seeds and things, and I got pretty much the same story that Mother had given me.

Leon obviously knew everything, and since he didn't introduce any new information about babies, I guessed that was all there was to it. So, due to lack of interest, I dismissed the whole boring thing.

*I*t was a January night, bitter cold. I had just been tucked into bed when there was a sudden flurry of excitement in the house. There were phone calls and a great deal of adult scurrying about taking place. Aunt Mae suddenly arrived.

Grandpa Bowman soon appeared from nowhere and swept Leon and me away in his Model-T. No one even said goodbye to us.

Soon we were at Grandma and Grandpa's house in Bethany, still in our pajamas. We were put to bed after a glass of milk and some of Grandma's yummy homemade bread and jelly. Whatever was happening back home, we weren't at all unhappy about where we were. Tomorrow we could help Grandpa feed the rabbits and chickens.

Meanwhile, back in Norman, Daddy had called Dr. Nielsen. Without announcing who he was, he blurted out, "Doctor, we're ready when you are!" and hung up.

Dr. Nielsen blinked herself out of a deep sleep. She dressed, picked up her bag, hurried to the door, and stopped abruptly. "Wait a minute!" she said aloud to herself. "Where is it I'm going?"

The doctor lived in a large, two-story house. Half of the first floor was her office, waiting room, and laboratory. She hurried into her office to check her book.

"It can't be the Williams baby—not due for a month yet. Not the Frank baby—that one's got five weeks to go. Hmm. Well, I guess it's Mrs. Sturgess that must be ready."

She drove to a wooden shack down by the water tower and knocked on the door. Strange—no lights. Mrs. Sturgess had averaged a baby almost every year for quite some time now, and being the stout peasant woman she was, the doctor usually didn't hear from her until after labor had begun. And then her fee for delivery was never more than one or two jars of home-canned vegetables or a scrawny fryer, or sometimes a loaf or two of homemade bread.

The door opened to reveal that Mrs. Sturgess had taken a year off. She wasn't even expecting.

"Ah, what's this? So now where is it I'm supposed to be?" she muttered, scurrying back to her car. "All I can do is go home and wait for someone to call me from where I didn't show up!" And her car roared off into the darkness.

Daddy had gotten Mother to the hospital, and the pains were coming fast. The nurses were preparing her as best they could, but no Dr. Nielsen. Soon they began pacing the floor along with Daddy. Still no doctor.

Dr. Nielsen sat dozing by the telephone with her bag in her lap. She jumped at the loud ring and grabbed the receiver.

"Hello? Hello? Who's this? Who's having a baby, and where are you?"

"It's John Frank, Doctor, and we're at the hospital. Grace Lee is just about to deliver!"

"Ah! The little stinker has jumped the gun!" she cried, slamming the phone on the hook. Her tone of voice said she was on her way.

It wasn't an easy birth. The contractions came and went for two days before there was an event that could be called blessed.

In addition to arriving five weeks sooner than expected, my sister would not wait for that last turn in order to make a traditional entrance into the world head first. We've since come to believe she was only backing up to get a good running start.

It wasn't the best position for poor Mother's sake, but in the early morning hours of January 11th, a tiny, screaming, red-faced bundle was rushed to the nursery with every nurse on duty in attendance. Incubators had not yet come into being, and premature babies had only a fifty-fifty chance at life. She weighed less than five pounds. Mother and Daddy dropped the "h" in John to make it more feminine and called her Joniece.

Head Nurse Duncan was a crusty old spinster who probably should have been a doctor. She had acquired more than enough knowledge, and certainly the experience, and was gruff enough that her orders were obeyed without question or hesitation. But her heart was golden, and her love for children kept her in the nursery many more hours than were required of her.

Stepping out onto the front porch of the hospital for a short break, she took a deep breath. It was cold, and the air smelled like rain was on the way. She turned to go back into the building when she heard a small cry. She looked around to find an orange crate on the hospital step filled with old rags. The rags moved.

She quickly scooped the wooden crate into her arms and scurried into the nursery. It was a tiny baby girl, apparently abandoned by a mother unable to care for her.

Nurse Duncan protected and doted on the child as if she had given birth to it herself, and later she was allowed to adopt the baby and raise her as her own. This baby was also called Joniece, as she was the second miracle in one night.

Joniece Frank, six months. 1938.

Leon and I stayed at Grandma and Grandpa's for two whole weeks before Mother was well enough to come home. Joniece was to stay at the hospital an extra week after that to ensure her chances of survival.

As small as my baby sister was, she was still bigger than either of my dolls, so I wasn't allowed to pick her up and play with her. But I liked to stand at her head and smooth her thick, dark hair. I wondered why hers was so black and mine was so yellow.

Oh well, I was sure to get another talk one day about seeds and things, and then the mystery would all be cleared up.

C H A P T E R   5

S oon it was apparent that my father's business needed community support to grow and thrive. But sadly, Norman didn't want us. The "town fathers"—the Chamber of Commerce and its various businessmen— made it quite clear that no manufacturer would receive their support. Norman, Oklahoma, was an educational community, and strongly discouraged industry. John Frank knew that while the business was still young, it had to be moved to another town.

My parents loved Norman. Lifelong friendships had been established, and they dreaded the thought of pulling up stakes and beginning again somewhere else.

Daddy went to several towns and approached their Chambers of Commerce. There were those who were openly rude and those who simply shrugged him off or ignored him. How could a little factory that made vases and things possibly be an asset to a town?

Of course the best clay was near Ada, and it would have been nice had Ada accepted us. But it seemed communities throughout the area were in agreement—a pottery company couldn't possibly be of any benefit to them.

"We're being told to move on," he would say. "And if we're to leave, there's a place we're supposed to go. I just haven't found it yet."

After much searching, he finally located a parcel of land east of Tulsa that he felt was suitable for a production plant. The land seemed adequate, and it was near a growing city, although Daddy hadn't gotten any "this is it" kind of feelings from looking at it. But time was running out, and he had to make a decision. One hundred dollars, most of the money that remained, was given as earnest money toward its purchase. It was Tulsa that would be our new home. Daddy started back to Norman with the news.

He made his way back through Tulsa to Highway 66 and headed southwest under a cloudy gray sky, wondering if he had done the right thing. Was Tulsa the place God really had in mind for him? He certainly didn't feel the way he thought he would when he gave the man his money.

He pulled off to the side of the road and turned off the engine. Staring straight ahead, tears began to well up in his eyes.

"Help me, Master," he cried, feeling very much alone. He rested his head on the steering wheel. "You know I want to do what's right. But I'm at my wit's end. I'm afraid now because I'm out of money, and I don't know if I did the right thing. I know I shouldn't be afraid, but I am! Help me, Master. Please show me what I'm supposed to do . . ."

Perhaps it helped lighten the weight in his aching chest to simply get the words out, but he did feel better.

He drove through the town of Sapulpa and was about to leave it behind when steam began to billow from under the hood of the car.

"Oh, no!" he moaned. "I forgot to fill the radiator before I got on the road, and it's boiling over again!"

Turning around, he found a small service station and grabbed the water hose. A young man appeared, and Daddy asked, "Mind if I leave my car here for a little while so it can cool? Maybe you can tell me where I can get a cup of coffee."

The boy pointed to a small hotel down the street and assured him it had a good coffee shop.

The buzzing neon sign read, "St. James Hotel Coffee Shop," and Daddy entered and sat down at the counter. It was mid-afternoon, and he was the sole customer.

A short, plump little man with a starched, white chef's hat came out from the kitchen and served him coffee, and they began to make conversation.

"You traveling through?" the little man asked with a heavy Greek accent.

"Yup, going back home," he replied blankly. "May I please have some water?"

"Oh, sure." The man turned and poured water from a familiar green pitcher. Daddy was not drinking.

"Whatsa matta, mista? You no like our good water?"

"Oh, the water's fine," Daddy frowned, making a face. "But that pitcher! Where did you get that awful lookin' pitcher?"

Nick Douvos straightened himself and didn't hide the fact that he was offended. "You no like dat porty pitcher? Let me tell you somethin', mista—thisa here pitcher got made by dis artist in Norman whoza gonna be famous man some day!"

Daddy blinked soberly, and Mr. Douvos continued his defense. "Looka dis nice green color. And it'sa nice shape, see? You crazy you no likea dis fine pitcher—made outta da clay from right here in Oklahoma!"

And Daddy's straight face broke into a hearty laugh. "Hold it, I love it! I'm the one who made that pitcher!" Offering his hand, he said, "My name is John Frank, and I'm sure glad to meet you."

Mr. Douvos blushed and reluctantly shook Daddy's hand. "Aw, Mr. Frank, you sure hadda me goin' there. Please—you call me Nick."

"I'm sorry I did that to you, Nick, but I couldn't help it. I had no idea I'd walk in here and find one of my pitchers on your counter. I sure needed a lift right now."

"Mr. Frank, my wife and me, we got three more your pottery at home. We love your stuff. Me, I wasa one time worka for da Waldorf Astoria in New York. I wasa salad chef a long time dere. We shoulda had a whole buncha dishes outta dis here. Woulda been beautiful!"

"Nick, you're very kind. But that's a little out of my class. Right now, I'm just trying to find a new location to build my factory. I've got to move out of Norman soon and . . ."

"Move? You lookin' for a place to move? So whatsa matta with dis town, Sapulpa? You tella me."

Daddy looked thoughtfully into his coffee and back into Nick's wide open black eyes. "Well, I ah . . ."

"You don't make no deals with no one yet, eh?"

"Well, as a matter of fact, I. . ."

"Here, Mr. Frank, you have another cuppa my nice coffee, and you don't go. I'ma gonna be back in a big hurry. You don't go nowhere!"

Off came the tall chef's hat, and Nick Douvos was out the door and scurrying down the street. Daddy sipped his coffee and laughed aloud, his hand coming down on the counter with a thud. After all, he had the place to himself, and for the first time in a long while he felt like having a good laugh. He got up and paced the aisle with his hands in his pockets before he sat down and took the last gulp of his coffee.

The door burst open. Nick was leading a well-dressed man whose friendly hand was outstretched. "I'm Mr. Cowden, President of the Sapulpa Chamber of Commerce."

"John Frank," he smiled, shaking his hand. "I'm pleased to meet you." And Nick was busy filling two clean cups with freshly made coffee.

"Nick tells me you're looking for a place to build a factory of some kind."

"He'sa make dis beautiful pitcher I got here on da counter, see?" Nick offered proudly.

"So you make pottery?"

"That's right, sir. I was head of the Ceramic Art Department at Norman for nine years, until I felt it was time to quit teaching and start doing," he explained. "I think I have a lot to contribute to a community, but Norman doesn't cater to industry. It seems they don't want me there if I persist in being a manufacturer."

Mr. Cowden looked thoughtfully into the young man's face and sipped his coffee. "Well, what is it you need to get started? What do you think it would take?"

Daddy silently talked away the nervousness welling up inside him. May as well shoot high. After a long pause he swallowed hard, looked squarely into Mr. Cowden's eyes, and smiled.

"I've got the know-how, and I've got the courage. What I need is around five thousand dollars and some support from the town. And in time, I can make you proud of Frankoma Potteries. You wouldn't be sorry, Mr. Cowden."

Hearty sandwiches were served by Nick who insisted that it was "on the house." The two men talked of possibilities for a location, about where he and his family could live, and what the community could do to help him begin. The Chamber of Commerce could perhaps help him buy some property, and maybe shares of stock could be sold to various businessmen to provide the initial capital.

At last the two men stood to say goodbye. "Looks like Sapulpa has a new resident," said Mr. Cowden as they shook hands warmly.

"Four," he corrected. "I have a wife and two little girls. But first I have to go home and talk this over with Grace Lee. She's my partner. I won't make a decision without consulting her first."

They parted, and Daddy stayed to say goodbye to Nick and thank him.

"Wait'll I go home and tella my wife! She gonna really be happy I met Mr. Frank whosa makea da nice pottery."

"Nick, you're sent from heaven," he beamed. "You may not understand that right now, but I'll tell you about it sometime. Goodbye, my friend."

The old Packard fairly flew back to Norman. That night, the story was unfolded to Grace Lee. "Honey, I feel so good about that town! You know, I'd no sooner finished asking for an answer, and I know it sounds crazy—but the car made me stop in Sapulpa. It works fine now. Didn't give me a bit of trouble on the way home! Can you beat that?"

Seeing that his old enthusiasm and drive had returned, Grace Lee had to agree that today the way had been shown. They would of course move to Sapulpa to begin a brand new chapter in their lives, and in their destiny.

CHAPTER   6

February, 1938. My sister was six weeks old when we packed our bags and boxes and headed for Sapulpa. Daddy was happy and fun again. He moved about so quickly that we all caught his enthusiasm. We drove into the driveway of our new home on South Main Street. It was another old, big house, and I recall the absence of a smile on Mother's face. But we were soon unpacking and making a home of it.

The house was made of dark red brick, and I remember thinking it looked like a big fat lady sitting in a large field of weeds. It sat heavily and looked very, very serious.

There was a big yard for me to play in, and Daddy promised to put a swing in the tall oak tree.

For a long time, I didn't see Daddy a lot. Grandpa Bowman came to live with us for several weeks, and he and Daddy got up very early every morning and took their tools with them, which Grandpa had lots of, because he was a preacher on Sundays and a carpenter on all the other days. Sometimes they came home long after I had gone to bed.

There was a lady who lived next door in a house that looked very much like ours, only bigger. It had a large screened-in porch with two wooden porch swings. I soon learned that she owned the house we lived in, too.

Behind her house were stables with horses. There were also chickens and ducks and guinea hens that had black and white polka dots and made funny screeching noises.

When Easter came, the lady brought me a mother hen and some baby chicks to care for. Only one chick survived. She was a Rhode Island Red. We returned the mother hen to the lady, but Little Red soon grew up and laid eggs for us every day. What a wonderful pet she became! She was a lot more fun than a silly old doll. Mother made her a little bonnet and an apron, and I took her for rides in my red wagon.

It was mid-summer when a young Indian girl came to stay with us in the daytime, as Mother was now helping Daddy. Catherine was fourteen. She loved to play with us, and we had picnics in the yard under the big tree with the swing. While Joniece and I took our afternoon naps, Catherine cleaned house and washed diapers and ironed. Daddy gave her three dollars every week.

Because Mother went with Daddy every morning now, we didn't see them a lot except on Sundays when we all went to our new church together. It wasn't like the one in Norman. This one was called "Methodist." I heard Mother say she didn't want her children to be brought up quite as strictly as she had been raised. Other than lots of new faces, the only difference I could see was that they were a lot quieter and didn't speak out so much while the preacher was talking. And that way he didn't have to talk so loud.

After church we would drive out to see what Daddy and Grandpa were so busy building. We drove to a place about a mile past the other side of town on Highway 66. There was one small building that had already been there which, once upon a time, had been a night club called "The Bucket of Blood." A man and woman were living there and at night watched the new building for Daddy. The new factory was being built about fifty yards to the south of the run-down old beer joint. The foundation was laid, and the walls were up. Soon there was a roof, and then a door Daddy could put a lock on. Daddy and a man who owned a truck then drove down to Ada to bring back the first load of clay (which he bought "dirt cheap," as he put it), to be used at the new Frankoma plant. And Daddy and Mother began making pottery.

The front of the old "Bucket of Blood" was used for showing the

Frankoma showroom. Sapulpa, Oklahoma, 1938. The Bucket
of Blood is converted into a showroom and living quarters.

pottery, and people driving by on the old two-lane Highway 66 would
stop and look. Sometimes somebody would buy something.

*S*eptember came. My summer braids were combed out and
made into Shirley Temple curls, and I began first grade at the
two-room school house a block away.

It was then that Daddy took me on his lap one day and hugged me
and said that it was time I started learning the value of money. He
gave me ten cents and told me that every Saturday I would get another
ten cents. "But," he added very emphatically (there was always a
catch), "the money we earn is never all ours. One-tenth of it belongs to
God, always."

This puzzled me somewhat. How would we ever get it to Him?
But I had no choice other than to go along with it. Nine out of ten
wasn't so bad.

"Every Sunday you'll put one penny into the Sunday School
collection plate. Then you can do anything you want with the other
nine cents."

There were warm hugs and kisses from both Mother and Daddy,
and visions of wealth danced in my head. I was swimming in fantasies
of what I could bring home from the dime store! Or maybe I would
save it.

I lay awake nights alternating between spendthrift and miser. As I remember, I started feeling taller. And sort of grown up. It would take a lot of thought and planning to make such weighty decisions as these, but the decisions would be mine!

10:20 P.M. on the night of November 10th, 1938. Our new telephone rang. Daddy answered, spoke a few words and threw his clothes on over his pajamas in panic. I heard Mother cry, "No, John! No! Not now!" And a pain that was altogether foreign to me stabbed my chest.

Mother stayed with my sister and me, while Daddy's car roared out of the drive toward the new plant that was already ablaze.

He and the people who lived in the little building fought the fire as best they could with what they had. But it was all going up in smoke. The fire department was called, but refused to respond because the plant was in the first block beyond the city limits. A few molds were saved, but it was considered a total loss. The cause of the fire was never learned.

In the days and weeks that followed, I listened to my parents talk. They said things like, "We mustn't be afraid, we've got to believe there's a reason for this," "We'll meet it with faith," and "Surely God knows what He's doing." I heard, but I didn't understand.

There were many prayers. We went to church regularly and, although food was not plentiful and my allowance was temporarily suspended, something was always put in my hand to drop into the collection plate as it went by. It was always a tenth of whatever we had.

Daddy told us no matter how hopeless things seemed, nothing good could happen if we were afraid—that fear of something happening could actually cause it to happen. But the business was gone—lost—and we would be homeless and hungry soon if a way was not found to begin again.

The townspeople who had bought stock in Frankoma when we first came to town did not want to invest more money in a down-and-out entity. And the local bank was out of the question because there was nothing to offer as collateral.

Some evenings Daddy would go and sit in one of the porch swings with the lady next door, and they would talk until after dark. But I was never allowed to go with him. I knew it had to be really serious talk, because every time he slowly walked back across the yard toward home, he had his hands in his pockets with his head bowed, his eyes to the ground. Sometimes I thought he was going to cry. Then he and Mother would sit in the living room and talk very low so I couldn't hear. But they didn't say very much.

They would then get up and hug each other for a long time, and sometimes Mother would kind of cry. Slowly they would climb the stairs and come to watch Joniece and me sleep for a while before they went to bed.

Sometimes I would cry then, too, because I was scared. I didn't even know why I was so afraid. But my chest ached, and I knew that things were really bad. I wanted to know what was happening so I could be a part of whatever it was that was so bad and cry with them. I tried to think of things to ask so they could maybe tell me. But I never could come up with the right questions.

One day Daddy went to Oklahoma City with the lady next door. When he came back the next day he was really happy. He smiled and laughed like things were going to get better. I think he must have talked her into buying stock or loaning him money or something so he could rebuild Frankoma.

Then Grandpa Bowman came with his big box of tools to live with us again for another few weeks. No matter how serious things were, Grandpa could walk in and laugh and make everything seem like it was all just a natural part of life's drama. Whenever he was there, the tensions of hardship were always relaxed, and things were fun again.

Grandpa seemed to know that even tragedy had a purpose. And that purpose was often to change the direction of our lives to turn us around and point us in the direction God meant for us to go in—the one that would lead to success, not failure. He repeated to us many times the story of a man named Job who never stopped loving God, no matter what hardships and tragedies he was given to bear.

$\mathcal{T}$he first of a new year came, and Mother and Daddy decided that we would move to the plant and live in the old Bucket of Blood. This way, Daddy could be near the plant and could keep a round-the-clock watch on the building himself.

It also meant that he could fire his kiln in the morning and get up during the night to check on it or turn it off. Mother could take care of Joniece and me and at the same time work the showroom and sell the pottery.

And so Dad went out with his ladder and paintbrush and repainted all of the signs at the Bucket of Blood to read "Frankoma Pottery," the name under which his company would operate from then on.

We took Big Red (formerly Little Red) to live at my grandparents' house in Bethany so she could be with the other chickens on the farm. It was sad for us to give her up, but we knew she would be happy with her new friends.

The people who had lived in the little building moved out, taking their several cats and dogs with them, but armies of fleas stayed behind to plague us for many long months afterward. They were in the cabinets, the baseboards, and in every piece of our furniture. We were often awakened by little things that went jump in the night.

Joniece and I slept on a double bed in a room on one side of the L-shaped little apartment. There was a small bathroom between us and the other half of the L which was a narrow living room and kitchen. Mother and Daddy slept in the living room on the studio couch, which doubled as our sofa.

Our little bathroom was also the public rest room. After each customer drove away, Mother would clean it thoroughly with alcohol so we wouldn't "get germs from strangers."

Our baths were mostly what we called "spit baths." But on Saturday nights after supper, Mother put a bucket of water and a teakettle on the kitchen stove to heat, and Daddy used pot holders and towels to carry them to the bathtub. Joniece and I were bathed first, and Mother used the water next. We tried to hurry so the water wouldn't get too cold before it was Daddy's turn.

There was always Sunday school and church the next morning, pick up the mail at the post office box, and then home to open the chicken-

wire gate that fenced in the "seconds" porch. That meant that
Frankoma was open for business. Sometimes there would be people
sitting in their cars waiting to come in.

Daddy was often criticized for not opening on Sunday mornings.
But he always responded with a good-natured smile. "Our church is
very important to us," he would explain. "And some day when we can
afford it, we'll close all day Sundays. I hope we didn't keep you waiting
too long."

Sometimes it got very busy in the showroom, and little Joniece could
not always be watched. She was only two years old, but she had the run
of the place.

One beautiful sunny Sunday, a couple entered the showroom and
announced that they were looking for a nude statue for their fountain.
Mother explained that we didn't make nudes. But they laughingly
insisted that they would be happy to take the one they had seen out in
front as they drove up.

Mother rushed outside to find that Joniece had disrobed and was
celebrating the warmth and beauty of the day by dancing for customers
as they came up the drive. And she danced divinely!

And so our former playmate, Catherine, was suddenly back the
following week to fill the principal roles of part-time babywatcher and
maid.

*M*other's artistic instincts for displaying the pottery quickly
turned to skill. Our life style left much to be desired, but
the product was selling. We even bought a new/old car for fifty dollars,
to be used as "the company car." It looked like a big black box on
wheels, but it ran loud and well.

Although the plant had been partially rebuilt and production was
rolling, sales were not enough to replace the necessary equipment and
materials that had been destroyed in the fire. And the money from the
lady on Main Street was gone.

No matter how hard Daddy tried to sell more stock, people were
disenchanted with the future of the pottery business in Sapulpa.

We were at lunch one day when, instead of just closing our eyes and asking God to bless our food, Daddy and Mother took our hands to form a circle around the table. I remember my father's strong and sincere voice as he asked the Master to go with him that day, that he knew he could say the right things if He would stay with him. Daddy then thanked his Heavenly Father as happily as if he had already heard Him say, "Yes."

We all kissed him and waved goodbye as he drove away in the direction of town.

"*G*uy, I have a plan," he said, beginning to outline it for the president of the bank. "I've shown you my books, and you can see that I was making a profit soon after the walls of my factory were up. With just Grace Lee and me and two high school boys working after school, we actually made a profit."

During the hours that followed, Daddy laid out his proposal. Guy Berry finally got up from his executive leather chair, stretched his back, and looked thoughtfully out the window.

"I don't have a lot of money," Daddy went on, "but what I have is all in your bank. I need some more to get going again, Guy. The fire really set me back. I've about got the building back together, but I need materials and equipment so I can produce. It's selling well enough, but I've got to produce more so I'll have something to sell."

Guy Berry was a banker, and bankers are not speculators. But he had listened kindly all afternoon to this young fool who had next to nothing and was shooting for the moon.

"But you have no collateral to speak of, John!" he argued, pounding the desk. "What do I have if you can't make the payments, just tell me that? A piece of a building?"

"You're investing in the town if you invest in me, Guy. Frankoma will put Sapulpa on the map one day!"

"Oh, come on, John. Stop talking like a star-struck kid. I can't deal in dreams. Give me something concrete!"

"You've got to believe in me. My plant can provide an income for as many as thirty-five or forty people some day! I'll bring money into this town! We'll be shipping all over the state in a year or two!"

Mr. Berry kept right on being a banker, and Daddy kept right on being a determined young dreamer.

Late in the afternoon, when the bank employees had long gone home and daylight was fading, the energy and determination of the young and foolish began to touch something in the old and established. Besides, Guy Berry was getting weary.

"Well, your books do look pretty fair, John," he said dryly. "I'll have to say you've looked all right as far as you've gone—which doesn't prove a damned thing, you understand!"

He looked out the window again and rubbed his five o'clock shadow. When he turned back, his voice was gruff and resigned. "Well . . . how much ya think you can get started on . . . "

They agreed on a sum and shook hands. Daddy was out the door when Mr. Berry called after him. "Remember! One day late on a payment and your goose is cooked!"

Mr. Berry walked slowly back into his office and put on his overcoat. Standing at the window, he watched the old black box turn the corner and head east.

"I must be outta my mind. What in the world have I done?"

CHAPTER 7

ecember, 1941. Pearl Harbor was bombed and war declared. Thousands of young men volunteered, some were drafted, and a few 4-Fs remained. In only a few months, Frankoma found no more than a few women to employ, plus two or three men who were either too old or too young to defend our country in WW II.

The new economy dictated that the small amount of money in circulation be spent for rationed food, rationed gasoline, and other absolute necessities. Few were buying pottery.

We wore shoes made of synthetic materials that used up our precious ration stamps and lasted scarcely half the period from one stamp allotment to another. Rather than ride the school bus, I asked for, and was given, an old bicycle to ride the two miles to school and back each day.

Despite the innumerable hardships and deprivation the whole country was forced to endure, Americans eventually began to loosen their purse strings once again. It seemed people were willing to stretch their budgets for an occasional extravagance, a bit of something nice to live with. Soon sales picked up again.

However, Daddy did have some shipping problems to overcome. New cardboard boxes were nonexistent during wartime, and who could have afforded them anyway?

Miraculously the old black car continued to run, and one day Daddy welded some rods together and made a carrier on the back of it. Before the sun rose each morning he went into town and drove up and down the alleys collecting any cardboard boxes he could find before the trash man came through.

As I was waking up to get ready for school, Daddy was coming home with boxes stacked in the rear carrier, the back seat, front seat, and tied to the top of the car. The familiar sight became known by the merchants in town as "John's Big Black Boxcar."

So, through most of World War II, pottery shipped from Frankoma arrived at its destination in Post Toastie boxes or Listerine cartons, and some were even marked "Kotex."

*B*ecause of the war, materials were frozen. Parts for machinery disappeared altogether for long periods. When a piece of equipment broke down in the plant, it took weeks or usually months to replace—if it could be ordered at all. In the meantime, Daddy had to fix what he could himself.

Although he was far from being a leader in mechanics, of necessity he became a great innovator. If he needed a machine to shortcut a process, he thought of a way to build it. Many of his early inventions were then unheard of in the manufacture of ceramics but, in years to follow, would be copied by his competitors.

Once the big stirring device in the mixer broke. It was a giant paddle that mixed the clay with water to wash it down and liquify it into "slip." The problem of repairing the vital part was assigned to three men. Production could not move without processed clay.

The three devoted the whole of the afternoon to determining just exactly what the problem was and how to go about solving it. Daddy returned at the end of the day expecting the paddle to be in working order, only to find them still standing around with pencils and paper.

He looked up at the tank, then at his men. Quietly and slowly he took off his belt. The men stepped back in disbelief that the bossman could be so angry that he'd actually strike them with his belt!

Daddy then quietly reached down, untied his shoes and slipped them off. His pants dropped to the floor, and in a moment he stood before the threesome stark naked. "Would you boys be good enough to hold the ladder for me? I'm going over the top and get to the bottom of this."

While the men relaxed and joked with relief, Daddy climbed over the top of the wall and dropped into the tank with a splash. He waded and crawled about in liquid clay up to his nose and got the paddle fixed and secured. When he was finished, he climbed back over the top of the tank wall and down the ladder, looking as if he were wearing a fitted grey body suit. Just then one of the lady trimmers entered the room and froze.

"Mr. Frank, are you . . . I mean where . . . Oh, Mr. Frank!"

Daddy called after her as she ran from the room. "It's okay, Bonnie! It's the only way I can play and not get my clothes dirty. Grace Lee would whip me!" And the men fell down laughing.

From that point forward, those three men became devoted to the bossman for whom no job was ever too dirty.

*F*rankoma's rutile glazes were different from anything else on the American market, or anywhere, and its line of original artware and sculpture was unique. But in order to put Frankoma "on the map," Dad and Mother knew they would

have to come up with something that could bring substantial volume sales.

The colors they produced already represented Oklahoma textures and terrains with Prairie Green, Desert Gold, White Sand, Onyx Black. But the design, as well, had to say, "This is Oklahoma."

So now my father and mother set to work creating a line of casual dinnerware with wide appeal, and in 1942, "Wagon Wheel" dishes were introduced. The set was offered in Prairie Green and Desert Gold.

Until that time, traditional tableware was primarily white, or white with colored designs added. But the design of these dishes was imprinted in the clay, and the colors were bold and daring. Soon Wagon Wheels was the rage. And Frankoma came to be recognized as the pioneer in colored dinnerware.

Daddy hired six new people to work in the plant. Each morning they gathered at the fire station in town and Daddy came to get them. They crowded themselves into the old black boxcar and were returned at the end of the day.

Soon Frankoma needed a bookkeeper, and a small desk was put into a corner of the showroom.

Mother took Joniece with her to the plant while she trimmed and sponged ware, with one eye always on the driveway for customers. I learned to push a janitor's broom and did my part after school and on Saturdays.

Soon there were twelve employees. Among them were a jolly little lady and her teenage son, of whom we all became quite fond. They were especially taken with little Joniece, who was developing into a delightful and entertaining personality, and she was just as taken with them. Maggie and Charles Henry often took her home with them to their farm on weekends. And when Joniece was there, she was "as happy as a puppy in a room full of rubber balls," as they would laughingly tell us. And all the while, Joniece was learning about cows and chickens and bunnies and birds and bees through the curious eyes of a child.

Portable potter's wheel. c. 1950.

$\mathcal{M}$ost traditional potter's wheels were motor driven, and required that one sit down to work at them, or more correctly "over" them. The revolving clay platform sat low into the "pan" surrounding it to catch the water that otherwise would have been slung out onto the floor while it was turning. By their very nature they were massive, extremely heavy, stationary pieces of equipment. Who had ever heard of a portable wheel?

But my father designed and built a unique potter's wheel especially for his traveling and speaking engagements. It was a wheel that allowed him to stand, not sit. The revolving clay platform was raised high above the pan so that what he was making could easily be seen by a large seated audience. Since he spoke in places in which he could not afford to leave behind a mess, he designed the clay platform so that it spun the water down into the pan, not out.

The unit was relatively light weight so it could be lifted in and out of a car trunk; it had a triangle of three castors on the bottom so it could be rolled about and in and out of buildings with ease; and it had only three pieces that could be assembled and set up in a matter of seconds, 1-2-3. Then with a mere flip of his finger, each castor popped up to the side, so that the three legs they were mounted on met the floor and stabilized the unit. The simple "kick wheel" he built into it was operated with one foot, made so that he had absolute perfect control of its speed, giving him the ability to perform many dramatic subtleties to visually punctuate important points in his talk.

Other businessmen carried brief cases. But Daddy's brief case was his wheel, and he never owned a car after that with a trunk it couldn't fit into.

*T*hen one day Daddy was invited to do a six-week tour to demonstrate on his potter's wheel at several large department stores throughout the eastern United States. It was to be very important publicity for Frankoma.

Joniece was only four and too young to really appreciate such a trip, my parents thought, so it was decided that she would stay with Grandma and Grandpa in Bethany. I, however, was taken out of school to go with them. They reasoned that it would be the experience of my lifetime, and equally as important to my education as school.

And so it was. New York, Boston, Philadelphia, Milwaukee, and Chicago. We traveled in our old Plymouth sedan and slept in many places called "tourist homes" that were far less expensive than hotels. It was wartime and, for two to four dollars a night, we could rent an extra bedroom (bathroom privileges included) in a private home; it was a time when everyone needed extra cash. I was very curious to see what real hotels looked like inside. But hotels cost far too much.

I became well traveled for a nine-year-old of that day. New York impressed me the most, and I had a strange awareness that I would one day return to Times Square. I saw myself as a grown lady, standing in that very spot watching the Camel man blow giant smoke rings across Broadway.

For many years afterward I would dream of going to live in New York City.

*F*rankoma's reputation began to spread throughout the state, and people drove long distances to see the new Oklahoma product. My father's personal popularity also grew as he continued to speak to more and more churches and civic groups, illustrating his message with his potter's wheel.

"This clay was just a hunk of mud when I found it sitting on a hill one day," he'd tell them, holding up a chunk of raw clay. *"I bought it for only a penny a ton, because it was worthless to anyone but me.*

"Ah, but I saw its value! I saw that it wasn't just dirt, but clay! And I know the difference, you see. It's this: clay has a 'life' in it that makes it quite special. Dirt falls apart—clay does not. It holds together so it can be molded and shaped into just about anything I wish it to be. It has potential—that's what makes it special! It obeys me, and I love this clay because it has personality and character.

"Now here's that same clay after it's been washed down with water and has had some of the impurities screened out of it." He would then take the ball of clay and place it on the platform. Dipping his hands in a bowl of water, he would drip a bit over the clay and start the wheel turning, his hands gently centering the damp earthen ball.

"You see, like this hunk of clay, I was worthless a long time ago. And the Master said, 'John, come with me. I'll show you how to be really worth something!'"

The ball of clay responded quickly in his skilled hands, and he kneaded it back and forth as the wheel turned, adding a little water from time to time to keep it workable.

"So I said, 'Okay, Master, you're the boss! Do with me what you will—I'm ready! I want to be something beautiful and useful, 'cause I'm sure not worth much sittin' on this hill doin' nothin'.'

"Then the Master took me in his hands and pushed me around a little and knocked some of the wind out of me," Dad would laugh, as he kneaded the remaining air bubbles from the clay.

And with only a light touch from his hands, the walls of a vessel began to rise. *"See? None of us is worth a nickel till we become clay in the Master's hands. But surrender yourself to Him—and see what He can make of you."*

As the wheel slowed to a stop, Dad would step back to study what he had just created.

"Now, that's a real nice crock, ladies and gentlemen. That's all some of us are—just good crocks. And those are sure nice to have around when you need them!"

The wheel made only a few more turns and, with a gentle touch, the shape and personality of the homely old crock was changed, as if by magic, to something much finer.

"We could stop here, you know. It's not so bad the way it is. I could quit now and have—mmm—maybe a five dollar vase." Then with a broad smile, he would continue.

"Ah, but the Master said, 'No, my friend, you've got more potential than that. Let's take you another step farther. Relax. Trust me.'"

Carefully he caressed the clay with movements of undetectable subtlety. In seconds, the character of the piece had been transformed, and the wheel again came to a gentle stop. With pride and pleasure, he admired his new creation.

"Now that, my friends, is a vozz!" he would exclaim, adding quickly, *"—that's a vase over ten dollars."*

Then came stories from the Bible about the many divine uses of clay. The very first, of course, was in Genesis when God made Adam from the clay of the earth. *"God was the Creator, and created me in His own image. He was the Creator—and so I have that inheritance!"*

Dad's favorite was in the ninth chapter of John. There was a man who had been blind from birth. The Master came up and spoke to him, then spit on the ground and made a bit of clay, which he put on the blind man's eyes and told him to go wash in the pool.

"I wonder what you or I would do if a stranger walked up to us and did such an awful thing! Here we are blind, and some

guy comes up and smears mud all over our eyes. Wouldn't we be a bit outraged?

"Ah, but this man heard the Master's profound and gentle voice and knew beyond all doubt that if he did as he was told, he would see. And so he did see! Because he obeyed the Master.

"How often do we not trust? Where is our faith when the Master speaks to us and tells us what we must do in order that we might see?

"Now, think about it. Wouldn't you like to be that little bit of clay? Wouldn't you like to say, 'Use me, Master—let me be that clay. Use me to open a blind man's eyes! Use me to open his eyes so that he may know You and see clearly for the very first time!'"

The wheel would begin again to turn. *"Some of us don't want to stop even when we get to be a 'vozz.' Some of us say, 'I think I can do even better than this, Master. Go ahead and try me.' So He pushes us even farther to see what we're really capable of."*

As he talked, one form quickly changed to another, and then to another, each more beautiful than the one before. Then ever so slowly and carefully he would put his hand into the top of the vessel and open the mouth of it, and in mere moments the walls would be outstretched, standing in mid-air with no support, like a fine plate.

He would now speak softly, as if the slightest noise could cause its collapse. *"I could let this sit overnight, and tomorrow it would be dry enough to fire and keep forever just as it is.*

"But, as you can see, I've worked this clay pretty hard, and it's mighty tired. You laugh? Oh, but it's true. One touch, you see (a light tap on the outer rim), *and it would collapse."*

The clay lay limp and exhausted, and it was obvious that nothing could be done to restore it, so he began to lovingly fold it back into a lump.

"You see, clay is very much like us. I can put a cloth over this, let it rest overnight, and tomorrow it will be ready to perform again. Clay will never die, you see. All it needs is a few hours of rest to restore its energies.

"So ask yourself—are you truly happy with your life the way it is? You may be sitting on a hill with the potential of being a fine china vessel. But you'll never know until you say to the Master, 'Lord, make of me what You will—I want to be something useful so I can serve.'"

He would often close by saying, *"Go home and sleep well tonight. Tomorrow the Master may call on you to do a very special job, and you'll want to be rested and ready!"*

John Frank loved people unconditionally, and they responded by returning that love. He more than just loved what he did. Being a potter was profoundly symbolic to him. It wasn't enough to show people how to make pottery. The joy that came from being a messenger and interpreter of the Divine Potter's teachings was not hidden under a bushel. It shone like a beacon over all who came to listen to him.

"If we don't pass it on, we don't get any more," he would laugh. "If we share it, it comes back to us a hundred times over. It doesn't work if you just talk about it, though. You gotta believe it with all your heart and soul and live it!"

If you are among the fortunate who knew his laugh, you can close your eyes this very moment and hear him. It was the genuine, undisguised sound of love. And its buoyant, effervescent quality never changed as long as he was with us.

During those years it was ever so difficult for Mother to be a mother and fill the many additional roles also demanded of her. It seemed as though she lived with one foot in our living quarters and the other in the showroom. Dad cut out a small window that looked from the kitchen to the showroom front door so she could watch for customers.

Often she would have to leave in the midst of washing or ironing or feeding Joniece to attend to customers. Joniece was not a patient child. She would vanish in a matter of seconds when left alone, and it often took a long time to return her to wherever she was supposed to be. The search would include the creek bank where she liked to catch

Family portrait. Sapulpa, Oklahoma, 1942.

grasshoppers in a jar, or the plant where she played beneath the casting benches. Sometimes we found her in the bathroom, having locked herself inside.

Mother performed a juggling act from morning until night. She was wife, mother, housekeeper, plant worker, sales manager and stock clerk, display artist, and office manager. She changed hats from minute to minute, at the same time trying to keep herself neat and presentable for the public.

There was one especially memorable day when Joniece was four. The showroom had become crowded with browsing tourists, and I was sent to get Dad from the plant to come and help. He was always covered with clay dust, but he never made apologies. Mother and Dad wrapped pottery while I ran back and forth to the plant for out-of-stock items.

Joniece rushed in and began tugging urgently at Mother's skirt, chattering excitedly. Mother was involved in a sale and told Joniece to go back into the house and wait until she finished.

She then ran to Dad and tried to get his attention. "Go back into the house, sweetheart, and we'll be right with you."

Her frustration mounted, and she returned to Mother. "Joniece," Mother said firmly, "go in and wait, and I'll be there soon. It can't be that important!" She turned her around and gave her an emphatic pat on the rear.

When all the customers had gone, Mother began looking for the little one to give her the attention she had demanded earlier. But Joniece had disappeared. She was not to be found in any of the usual places, and an all-out search began. Several men from the plant were even summoned to help look for her.

An hour later—Mother in tears—Joniece was found a mile north on busy Highway 66, walking and sobbing, a photograph of Mother in one arm and a Bible in the other. She was running away from home because no one loved her.

It was so melodramatic it was almost impossible not to laugh. But she was genuinely hurt, and Mother and Dad knew it. They held her for hours, stroking her, talking to her, and pouring all the love and caring into her they could.

"She needs more of my attention, John," said Mother, rocking Joniece in her arms. "We're going to hire a part-time girl in the showroom. We simply must now." And it was done.

CHAPTER 8

For Frankoma, things got worse before they got better. Although Mr. Berry at the bank was receiving each monthly payment promptly, the lady on Main Street saw less return on her investment. She was a kind person and quite fond of my father, and although she understood the problems he faced, she was also a businesswoman. And as time went on, both her husband and her business manager urged her to foreclose on Frankoma. She prolonged procedures until she could no longer withstand the pressure. She finally conceded.

I remember my father standing outside the door and refusing to let the boards be nailed up and the sign posted. Frankoma would remain open for business. The sheriff's men came at night to perform their duty while he was asleep. But Dad slept lightly, listening for an approaching car that could bring the signs of his defeat, and he stood his ground.

Almost a month went by, and the doors of Frankoma did remain open for what little business there was. Mother and Dad were quieter than usual, I thought, and we continued living even more frugally than before.

No matter what else we had to forego, there was always gasoline to get us to Sunday school and church. And through it all, never once did my parents refer to the lady on Main Street in a cross or derogatory way.

Then one afternoon the lady on Main Street walked through our front door. For the very first time, it was she that came to my father.

"John, just what the devil do you think you're trying to prove?" she demanded, waving her silver-handled cane. "My attorneys tell me you refuse foreclosure, and I came here to tell you it can't be done. The law is the law!"

Dad smiled and shrugged his shoulders. "Well, we're still open for business, aren't we?"

The lady sat down in disbelief and dabbed her face with a linen hanky. She looked at Dad's childish grin, and her own face began to soften. "John," she said shaking her head, "what am I going to do with you anyway?"

It was a serious business errand, but it was obvious they respected and understood each other perfectly.

Dad bowed grandly to her as he assumed a new role. "Allow me to show you through my pottery plant, Madam," he offered ever so graciously. "I know it doesn't look like much now, but just wait until you see what I have planned!" And while he continued to talk, he proceeded to lead her out the front door toward the plant. The lady was wide eyed at his audacity.

"You see, we plan to expand soon now, and over on this side will be the new casting department. Then we'll need another kiln or two, of course, and we'll have to make room for it by moving our glaze department back closer to the clay shed, and . . ."

"Now, just a minute, John!" she interrupted. "You're pretending you know where all this is coming from. Why, you can't even . . ."

Dad chuckled and shrugged. "My dear lady, the Lord is good to those who work for Him. And I know that this is what He means for me to do, and He'll show me how to get there. He sent you to me, didn't He?"

She eyed him suspiciously. "John, I came here . . ."

"You've never seen how pottery is made, have you?" he continued with a flair. "Let me show you how I often create an original before it goes into production."

Reluctantly the lady followed him to the rear of the plant where the potter's wheel stood. Dad picked up a piece of clay and pounded it several times between his palms. He then placed the ball of clay on the wheel and centered it. Her attention focused on the turning wheel as if she were hypnotized. As the clay responded in my father's hands, the lady's firmness melted into childish delight at the miracle she was witnessing.

"This one is especially for you, dear lady," he declared grandly, "with love." And he meant it.

Minutes later the wheel slowed to a stop, and she gasped in amazement. "John! It's perfectly beautiful!"

"It's one of a kind, you know. There will never be another like it. I'll let it dry tonight, then tomorrow I'll glaze and fire it. As soon as it's finished, I'll drive out and bring it to you," he promised. He offered his arm to her and said, "Now may I show you around the rest of my plant?"

Slowly they walked through the factory as my father explained each step of the process from clay to finished product. The lady nodded her head and listened with interest for nearly an hour.

Outside the door, the lady stopped and studied my father's face. "John, I have a confession to make, and I don't know what you'll think of me." Her eyes then looked away to avoid his. "You've met my husband. He's a good person, but he's . . . well, he's the way he is."

She took a deep breath and sighed. "And then there's my business manager. Heaven knows with all the money my first husband left me, I need a full-time helper to look after my investments. I've hired him to advise me, and he does his job well."

They began to stroll in the direction of her car. "But I sometimes listen to them when I shouldn't." Now the lady stopped and looked at him squarely. "You know I'm Christian Science, John. And I've admired your spunk when you were running on nothing but faith and guts. I like that!"

They resumed walking. My father remained silent with his hands clasped behind his back, listening.

"And no matter what," she declared, "I still have the final say in my own affairs." Soon they stood at the door of her car.

"John . . . I'm signing the plant back over to you. It's yours. It always has been and, God willing, it always will be."

Dad swallowed hard and slowly shook his head. "The Lord sure works in strange and mysterious ways," he said under his breath.

The lady shrugged. "Now, what in the world do you suppose I'd want with a pottery plant anyway? I'd only have to turn around and hire you to run it, and that wouldn't make either one of us very happy, now would it?"

Her driver opened the door and helped her into the back seat. "Get in, John, I'm not through," she commanded in a parental tone.

My father sat beside her as she wrote. "Here's something to help you over this rough spot you're going through." She folded the check, put it into his hand, closed his fingers around it, and gave his fist a decisive pat. "Now you'd better get to work if you're going to get that new casting department built. I have a feeling it won't be long before the business starts pouring in."

The lady relaxed and looked at him thoughtfully. "You're a rare breed, John. You've got what it takes. You'll make it."

My father stood with blank face and watched until her car was out of sight. He clutched the paper in his hand and walked slowly through the showroom and into the kitchen where Mother was preparing dinner. Dazed, he slumped into a chair at the table.

"John, what is it?" asked Mother, fearing the worst. "Honey, don't look that way. What's happened to you? Say something, John. Please! Are you all right?"

Dad handed her the piece of paper. "Tell me what it says. I can't look."

Mother opened it and read slowly. "One thousand, five hundred dollars . . ."

They looked at each other, and all their love was in their eyes. There was a long embrace, and the tears flowed without shame.

"Grace Lee, we've been given another chance. Thank you, Master! We're so grateful to You for making this possible."

It was the last time we ever saw the lady on Main Street. She passed away soon afterward.

Had she been sent especially to reward my father's faith?

Yes, she had been sent. And she played her role splendidly.

*W*ord traveled fast that Frankoma was still open for business, and people began to come in droves.

A secretary was hired, and she and Mother traveled to the Dallas Wholesale Gift Show the next spring and fall. Pottery samples were displayed on two shelves of unfinished boards, a couple of chairs, and still others were spread over twin beds in a small room at the Adolphus Hotel.

By the time Joniece was five, she spent much of her play time in the plant. She waited for the casters to take pieces from the molds and picked up the trimmings from the floor. When she had collected a sufficiently large ball of clay, she would find a corner in the clay shed and do her own creating.

One day she cut out of *Life Magazine* a picture of a circus clown and shaped his funny head with a ball nose and hat and clown makeup. It was such a good likeness that Dad showed her how to carefully glaze it with a brush in three colors, and it was fired.

Each evening after supper, Dad walked over to the plant to check the kilns. Joniece was almost always with him, holding his hand and skipping along beside him. All her thoughts of the future included, "I'm going to be like Daddy and be his helper some day."

She fantasized being a potter as her hero held her up to a small hole in the red hot kiln where she could see the melting cones. It fascinated her. And she asked questions, lots of questions. Her questions were advanced for her age, and Dad patiently answered each one to her satisfaction. After we went to sleep, Dad and Mother would muse over the things she had asked.

Joniece watched the casters pour slip into the plaster molds and wanted to know where the molds came from. So for a period of time we knew to look for her first in the mold shop. Time after time she watched the plaster being mixed and poured and the pieces taken apart and put back together, held with large rubber bands Dad had made by cutting old inner tubes into half-inch strips.

Then for the next few weeks we knew to look for her in the jigger department where she studied how the plates were made, in the days before the jigger wheel was replaced by the hydraulic press. Lumps of clay were smashed with a large heavy plaster weight to make clay "pancakes," then slapped onto a mold that sat on a motor-driven wheel. The jiggerman would pull down an arm that was cut like the edge of a huge key. When that patterned edge dug into the spinning clay, the bottom of the plate would appear, flinging strips of excess clay onto the floor and all about. In only a few seconds the plate was set on a shelf to dry.

Whenever a group of visitors came to tour the plant, Joniece tagged along and listened, and soon she had the whole story down pat. She envisioned herself one day showing people through the factory, explaining to them how pottery is made, and knowing all the answers to the questions they would ask.

Unlike the rest of us, my sister never daydreamed about being a nurse or a secretary, or whatever other traditional female role. There was never question about her future. Frankoma was to be her life, and nothing ever dissuaded her from that ambition.

Dad was confident, even at that early age, that Joniece was his heir to Frankoma.

One day it occurred to me that Joniece would enter school in just one year, and I was alarmed at the prospect of her being an ordinary first grade student. So I set to work teaching her the alphabet and, if she showed promise, I planned to throw in a bit of arithmetic. She would have a glorious head start and probably skip a grade in no time at all.

"A," I began.

"B," holding up the cards I had made.

"Ceeeee!" I shouted when she cried tears.

Joniece was far from being a model student. Clearly, she didn't lack intelligence, but her attention span for school work was five to ten minutes at the most, and that was on her good days. Within a year we got up to "R" and as far as 3 + 3. I was sure she would suffer because I had failed to prepare her, and I felt pangs of guilt when she finally began school.

That same year, however, I was distracted by a startling and pleasant discovery of my own—boys! They were different. And so the whole world began to look different to me. My extraordinary little sister could probably muddle through somehow without me.

C H A P T E R   9

ork at Frankoma Pottery began promptly at 7:30 A.M. The liquid clay was put into spouted coal buckets and carried to the casting department to be poured into molds. Even some of the women lifted the heavy pails and cast until noon, then trimmed and sponged ware or stacked kilns in the afternoon. Some workers doubled as glazers or scraped molds until cleanup and time to go home at four.

One day Dad went to town and came back with a kitchen timer for the mold shop. It had a little bell that signaled when the plaster had set just exactly long enough. This revolutionary gadget was a treasure to him, and he justified the three dollars he splurged for it in the name of progress. It freed him to do other things while the plaster was setting, and there was no more guesswork as to precisely when it was ready.

I remember hanging around the mold shop after school watching the little dial, anticipating the magic "ding" that would propel Ed and

Leona and Dad into the swift motions of pulling apart and trimming the clean white plaster molds.

The old gas stove was not large enough to heat the entire building in winter, but its efficiency was much improved when Dad hung some crude tin vents over it, which slowly carried some of the heat to other areas of the plant.

Leona and Betty often arrived a few minutes early in the morning and prepared a large pot of beans, and the top of the old stove got just hot enough to cook them to perfection by noon. Mother brought a loaf of bread and some margarine, and lunch became a feast for all the Frankoma family. But we never ate a bite before Dad said a prayer of thanks for all this abundance.

There was always a party at Halloween. Dad traditionally "forgot" to shave for a few days before and dressed as a bum with baggy pants and big suspenders. Everyone came in crazy clothes, and a nonsense prize was given for the best costume.

At the Christmas season, the Frankoma employees busily gathered clothing from their own closets, as well as from their neighbors, friends, and relatives. Children's toys were bought and made. Each person brought a can or two of food from their own kitchen. And whatever loose change they had in their pockets was put into a big jar, which was used to buy a big turkey and all the trimmings. When it was all neatly packaged, it was delivered to a needy family who would not have otherwise had a very festive Christmas.

After the food and all the gifts had been delivered, then came our own holiday parties. There was a party in the afternoon for the employees' children. Then the grownups' party at night was a big affair. There was much celebrating and singing of carols. People were filled with the spirit and, it seemed to me, it was what Christmas was all about.

My father knew the importance of sharing what we had, no matter how great or how small, with others. And he encouraged his employees to adopt the good habit of giving. In the early years, Frankoma's entire contributions often filled only one or two cardboard boxes. But as the company grew, eventually a truck was required to deliver all the food and presents that were given to the family Frankoma adopted at Christmas. And under Joniece's leadership, the tradition of giving continued for many years after he was gone, and the many people whose lives they touched "passed it on" as well.

Even in the early days, we had a get together every few weeks in our back yard for the employees and their entire families; or in winter we used the kiln room where it was warm. Mother and Dad usually made a huge pot of chili. There were plates of celery and carrots and olives and lots of crackers and good bread to go with it. Getting together for fun away from the job became an event that all looked forward to.

It seemed my father never missed an occasion to show his appreciation for his employees. Even on Valentine's Day, Dad assumed the role of a romantic young man, and every lady that worked for him was personally presented some candy. In the early years, it was only penny candy. But eventually, as he could afford it, the gifts evolved to boxes of fine chocolates.

No one was ever reprimanded for having fun on the job at Frankoma. On the contrary, it was encouraged. Dad said that work wasn't work if you enjoyed what you were getting paid to do. And that's the way it was. People worked hard for my father, yes. But he loved and appreciated them, and he was not ashamed to express it freely. He may have been the bossman, but he was also their friend.

When there was a dirty or tough job to be done, he did not stand aside, telling his employees what to do and how to do it. He was in the thick of it, working alongside them, actively helping with the work at hand.

Mother and Dad were also busy with church work—teaching Sunday school and singing in the choir. Mother's voice was like an angel's, and we were so proud. Sometimes she sang a solo, and many came especially to hear her.

Dad sang tenor. The truth was that he had a bass voice, but as always, he went where he was needed and did the best he could. The choir was always short of tenors.

He was now accepting many more invitations to speak to service organizations and church groups, as long as they didn't interfere with his own church duties. He could pay his own way now, and he never accepted money for his speaking engagements—except when he had to drive considerable distances, and then he asked only for gasoline expenses.

Dad loved to speak to people, particularly young people reaching what he called the "decision-making age," the teens. His own teenage years were admittedly the most important and formative years for him. And it was important to "pass it on" as early in life as the message could be heard and understood.

My father's occupation was clearly his life's testimony to the Divine Potter, and the art of pottery making took on a new meaning for young people everywhere. There before them stood a living example of what the principles of Christian living were all about. They worked. People witnessed the enthusiasm and joy with which he lived his life. And he passed it on to thousands.

"Why just get by in life when you can take the Master with you? Then you're traveling first class!"

Being a member of the Rotary Club was also very special to him, and he was very proud to belong. He took very seriously the challenge of "the four points" and practiced them religiously throughout his life, asking with each decision he made: Is it the truth; is it fair to all concerned; will it build good will and better friendships; will it be beneficial to all concerned?

1945 The Salvation Army asked my father to serve on its Board of Directors, and there followed many years of rewarding hard work in its administration.

Every Christmas season would find Dad on the street corner in the traditional Salvation Army booth in front of the dime store, ringing the bell, laughing, and calling out a hearty "Merry Christmas!" and "God bless you!" to passers by. Those whom he did not know knew him, and they dropped their money into the big red pot. He always came home cold and exhausted, but laughing at the good time he'd had. Often we tried to persuade him to let someone else stand in the freezing weather, and he'd say, "Naw, can't ask someone else to do something I won't do myself!"

Dinnerware patterns (top to bottom): Mayan-Aztec, Wagon Wheels, and Oklahoma Plainsman.

y 1946, Frankoma had become the leader in colored dinnerware. The Wagon Wheel dishes had been so successful, it was time to go forward and expand on a good idea. So two more patterns of tableware were introduced that year.

While still in Norman, Dad had put into line a pitcher, cups, sugar, and creamer that featured a Mayan-Aztec pattern. Mother thought it would be smart to use that theme and expand those few pieces into a full set. And it was done. This pattern lended itself well to almost any color, so along with Prairie Green and Desert Gold, it was made in White Sand.

The Mayan-Aztec and Wagon Wheels were obviously "theme" sets with a lot of design. Dad wisely decided that the third pattern should appeal to people with more streamlined tastes. The round plate he designed had four evenly-spaced indentations on the rim, which he called a "round square," and all the accessory pieces would follow suit. What better name for the plainest of patterns than "Oklahoma Plainsman?" New colors were also to follow, and eventually the Oklahoma Plainsman pattern of dinnerware was offered in virtually all of Frankoma's Southwest colors. Mother wasn't always pleased with the way food looked on some of the colors, but popular demand overruled her.

All colors that Frankoma developed were represented in nature in the Southwest. In addition to Prairie Green, Desert Gold, White Sand, and Onyx Black, there were Woodland Moss, Redbud, Clay Blue, Sunflower Yellow, Robin Egg Blue, Peach Glow, Brown Satin, and Flame.

Frankoma dinnerware was made for the most part in colors that enhanced food and made it look appetizing, a feature that Mother insisted on. It was durable, ovenproof, and the price was still reasonable enough that virtually everyone could afford to own it, standards that Dad insisted upon.

"What's the point of making pottery only a few can afford," he reasoned, "when we can produce a product we can price low enough for everyone to own?" And that's why he had worked so hard to develop and perfect the one-fire process unique to Frankoma. It was simply much cheaper to manufacture his product.

Over a bowl of soup one day, the idea came to Daddy to put a handle on the bowl. "Why not? Am I the only soup lover that likes to drink his soup?" To our knowledge, John Frank was the inventor of the "soup cup," an item soon afterward copied by tableware companies the world over.

Throughout the 1940's, clay was still being hauled from Ada in an old sideboard truck that was hired, along with a driver and one other man. My father always accompanied the dig, because selection of the clay was crucial. The trip often took two days, and they camped out at night at the site. Wrapped in blankets, they slept on the ground.

Driving home, Dad could have ridden the whole trip in the cab of the truck, because he was the bossman. But he always insisted on trading with the other two men, riding his share outside, bouncing around on top of the pile of clay in the back.

There was an especially hot day once when the truck rolled into the driveway. Dad climbed down from the clay pile covered with mud and dust from his head to his shoes. His hair stood straight up where the wind had left it, and his face was crimson and blistered from the sun.

Mother ran out excitedly to meet him. "Governor Phillips is waiting to see you, John . . ." She stopped short and turned pale when she saw him. "Good heavens, honey—you can't go in looking like that!" she gasped. "What are you going to do?"

Dad laughed and proceeded toward the showroom with long strides. "Oh, I'll just dust myself off a bit . . ." he shrugged, slapping his trousers and sending clouds of clay dust in all directions.

"Governor Phillips, it's a pleasure!" he said holding out his hand, not even offering an apology. The two men laughed heartily, strode into the office together and sat down.

"What can I do for you, my friend?"

The two were as friendly and comfortable with each other as if they had spent years in the clay pile together.

Mother slumped into a chair outside the office door and sighed. "I'll never worry again about whether or not his tie is on straight."

But their friendship grew, despite my father's unkempt appearance, and Dad was soon commissioned to design Governor Phillips' personal gift for each member of the Governors Conference in Washington, D.C., that summer. It was an ash tray with an impression of the Oklahoma state seal taken from the gold doorknob on Governor Phillips' office door at the state Capitol.

Other special orders began to come in from various big industries across the state for executive gifts and company awards. Frankoma was finding its way into offices and reception rooms all over Oklahoma, and people began to recognize it by name because of the unique designs and distinctive colors Dad was developing.

When the Broadway show *Oklahoma!* opened and became an instant hit, each member of the cast received a set of Frankoma dinnerware as a personal gift from Governor Roy Turner. The plates carried the signatures of all the members of the original cast.

Governor Robert S. Kerr made certain that every governor in all forty-eight states was reminded of Oklahoma and its creative use of natural resources by presenting each of them with a set of Frankoma dinnerware.

Frankoma Pottery. Sapulpa, Oklahoma, 1947. Frankoma ships
a set of dishes to each governor, as a gift from Robert S. Kerr.

*T*he summer I graduated from grade school, our whole family
graduated to a new/old house in town. It was across the street
from the high school. I was to attend junior high only a few blocks
away, and Joniece could walk to the nearby grade school. And at last
we began to know a bit of comfort.

The war was nearing an end, and Dad set up a training program for
GIs at Frankoma. Mother stayed home now to be a mother and
housewife. But in only six months, Dad implored her to return to the
plant and do what only she could do with such skill and finesse—
display and sell Frankoma. No one he could hire at any price could
approach her talent for arranging and grouping and showing the
pottery to its greatest advantage. He could manufacture, but he needed
his other half—the seller of his wares.

Although Mother felt she was needed at home to take care of Joniece
and me, she agreed to return if she could hire someone to help with the
family maintenance. And dear Viola came to us.

Viola was a hardworking and cheerful lady who came three half-days
a week to wash and iron and do some of the housework. We loved her
and came to depend upon her in so many ways. And Mother went back
to work at Frankoma during the hours we were in school.

The business continued to grow, and Mother and Dad were exhausted when they came home in the evenings. But it was a good tired, because the pottery was being created, and the pottery was being sold.

If customers asked about the making of pottery, Dad dropped everything and gave them a guided tour, often throwing a piece on the potter's wheel for them. Dad's personal demonstrations soon became a special feature of Frankoma factory tours, and teachers brought busloads of children to see pottery made. They took the message home, and word spread. Parents and families returned and bought Frankoma.

Salesmen were taking the line, and pottery was being shipped to wholesale accounts in several states. GIs came home, and new employees were hired.

By 1948, the plant needed to expand in order to produce enough to meet the new demands. This time Guy Berry was happy to loan the funds.

Finally our future was beginning to feel a bit secure.

*F*rankoma's books were at last seeing a healthier-than-ever black, instead of red. And my father's earliest conceptual ambitions were being realized—creating a product that people wanted to live with, at a price everyone could afford to pay.

"If you just want something to eat off of," he'd say, "then go buy a pie tin. It'll hold lots of food and probably won't even leak. But ahhh," he'd smile proudly, "if you want something to enhance the food and make your meals more pleasurable, try eating from one of my plates!" And people did. By the hundreds.

Frankoma was now becoming an attraction beyond Sapulpa, and the Oklahoma State Chamber of Commerce was forced to take a serious look. Never had an industry attracted so much tourist traffic to the site of the creation of its product. They hardly knew how to label it, and they haggled over a category in which to place it. For Frankoma did not *supply* a market, but rather *created* one, with new products, colors, and ceramic concepts, all from the unlimited but unnoticed clay in the hills of Oklahoma. It was unique.

Tulsa's Philbrook Art Center honored my father by making him the first commercial artist ever to be given a one-man show.

On November 10, 1951, a letter was received from the International Ceramic Museum of Faenza, Italy, requesting several pieces of Frankoma for a permanent exhibit representing American artists. His works in Faenza would be in good company—Picasso, Matisse, Leach, Kage, Kreps, Lundgren, and others. John Frank was beginning to be recognized as the artist he was.

It was a happy occasion when a selection of his works was crated and taken to the terminal bound for Italy. As my father stood on the loading dock, we felt the importance of the moment well up in him, causing him to turn his face away. We watched the crates being loaded onto the freight car, and we didn't take our eyes off the train until it was out of sight. Faenza, Italy! Now Europe would know him, too.

*B*y 1950, the Frankoma showroom had outgrown the little building that was once a wayside beer joint, and Guy Berry said, "Go ahead and write the checks, John. I'll cover you."

Plans for the addition were drawn and redrawn. Finally, it was settled. The new showroom and offices would be built on the north side adjoining the factory. There were months of construction that followed.

It then became imperative that Frankoma be reorganized into two corporations, separating manufacture and sales. My mother fought accepting the overwhelming responsibility of the sales corporation, but Dad insisted that she was not only capable, but was the only person who could do it.

It was the first time I can remember the presence of conflict between my parents. But it was a giant decision for my mother to make, and several times I heard her crying. I knew it was fear she wrestled with, the fear of commitment to such an enormous responsibility.

One afternoon I walked in through the front door to overhear her saying, "All right, John . . . if I'm going to do it, I'm going all the way, so just watch my dust! I'm tired of struggling and worrying about how

I'm going to pay the bills. I'm sick of being poor! So just stand back, because *I'm going to make money!*"

I stood at the door and saw my father embrace her tenderly while her relief came in a flood of tears.

"I love you, sweetheart," he whispered, comforting her. "You won't be sorry, I promise. I'll make you the richest lady in the world. You deserve the very best, and I'm going to give it to you." And tears were coming from his eyes, too.

All at once I felt like an intruder in an intimate love scene. I turned and tiptoed quietly out the door.

*I*n the months that followed, Mother set up her office and moved fiercely toward the organization of her new corporation. There was a sales force to hire and train; the display room needed scores of flower arrangements and several tables of dinnerware; there was an accounting system to set up and files to make. She needed a staff she could depend on, and she screened her applicants carefully. Finally several hundred letters were sent out announcing the opening of the new retail facility.

Mother and Dad were overwhelmed when several florist trucks arrived with potted plants and large bouquets of congratulations. They received telegrams from several states. Cards and letters poured in from everywhere.

New signs went up on the highway, and people came to see the new showroom and buy Frankoma Pottery.

CHAPTER 10

e were proud of my father's achievements and awards. Besides being the head of a growing company, he worked tirelessly for his church and the Salvation Army. He served both local and state chambers of commerce and traveled throughout Oklahoma speaking to churches and youth groups. And still he felt he was not doing enough. His loyalty was not limited to community and state, and he felt he needed to be involved on a national scale.

It was the beginning of a nightmare for us all as a family. We were to watch him extend himself beyond all limits in the name of patriotism and loving service until he was humiliated and despised by many who once called him friend.

It was during the era that all America was looking suspiciously behind doors and under beds for communists. And my father jumped into the fight to protect America from the threat of communism. He solicited funds and, with much of his own money, helped found an organization known as The American Patriot.

A newspaper press in Illinois was bought and shipped piece by piece to a location on Main Street in Sapulpa. It was, when reassembled, the third largest press in Oklahoma, taking its place in line with the *Oklahoma City Times* and the *Tulsa World*.

It was capable of printing a half-million tabloids in four-color process in just eight hours, although it would never be called upon to prove its capacity. And with that machine, The American Patriot began printing a newspaper that carried stories and information to bolster America's strength by promoting its free enterprise system and constitutional principles.

There were many organizations and churches and private citizens that supported The American Patriot by their donations and subscriptions to its publication. But its appetite for money was never satisfied, and the organization remained financially weak. Although money was borrowed to the limit and donations collected to keep it alive, Frankoma remained its primary source of funds.

The American Patriot consumed my father's days and nights until we rarely saw him except when he came home to bathe and change his clothes to leave for another meeting. We especially missed him at mealtime. The food never tasted quite as good without him there to ask the blessing.

Time passed, and Grace Lee herself finally reached the breaking point. All her energies were going into marketing Frankoma, and the money was coming in. But the money was rapidly going out, devoured by the insatiable monster already waving a flag of defeat.

There was no doubt as to the message on the wall. The American Patriot—i.e., John Frank—had bitten off more than he could chew alone. And in the end he was virtually that—alone. We saw him financially drained, and he eventually became so deeply wounded emotionally that we all felt his pain and begged him to "come home."

But how could he have done it any other way? Big was the way he thought. Whenever there was a cause he could support, he got behind it with all the force and energy he could muster. It was the way he was.

Dad had been so caught up in protecting the country's free enterprise system that his own beloved enterprise was going down the river. My mother knew it was time at last to put her proverbial foot down and bring him to his senses.

It was after supper one evening that she begged him to sit down and listen to what she had to say. They talked for a long time before Mother collapsed into an armchair and leaned her head back in exhaustion.

"John, you know I have always supported you in everything you've undertaken. But let's stop and take a look at our lives.

"Through all these years, promoters have come to us with all kinds of gimmicks, and we always bit because we needed to make the money. In all those things we let people talk us into doing, we lost money every single time. And now this American Patriot! Have you forgotten that we're artists? What has happened to the dream, John?"

Mother shook her head slowly. "Honey, we haven't enough money in the bank to pay our grocery bills, and we have no more credit. Now, tell me how I'm supposed to feed the four of us!

"Don't you see that every single time we've gotten away from employing *our* ideas and doing projects that are our *own*, we get into trouble and lose?" she demanded tearfully.

"Please come back to Frankoma and give up trying to save the world. You simply cannot continue to perform two full-time jobs at once," she pleaded. "Please come back to Frankoma where you belong. We need you so . . ."

Dad looked at her sad eyes and saw in them what he had been overlooking. He could not argue with her. He was tired too, and he lowered his head in a gesture of defeat.

"You're right, Grace Lee. I've tried so hard. But you're right as always."

He took her hand in his and kissed it. "I've put a terrible burden on you, and I'm so sorry. Will you ever be able to forgive me? I'll try and make it up to you somehow."

My father embraced her tenderly. "You know how much I love you. You'll always be my sweetheart."

The wounds were not to heal immediately. But my father would not dwell on the past or harbor guilt and regret. It was not without effort, but he held his head high. "The important thing is not whether you're right or wrong," he was often quoted as saying. "If you feel deep in your heart that what you're doing is right, even God himself doesn't expect more of you than that."

Although Dad's patriotic venture was a failure, as most of us judge and measure failures, he never regarded it as such. He saw it as another "lesson" that the Master had brought him through to prepare him for something that was to come. And it always amazed me to learn again and again that it was invariably just that.

It was a long struggle to recuperate from the bankruptcy of The American Patriot. There were legal merry-go-rounds, bureaucratic red tape, and court battles to be fought. And for well over a year it took its toll on both my parents.

The press was eventually sold for the best offer, a mere fraction of its worth and what was owed on it, but it was good riddance.

Frankoma slowly began to get back on its feet. It was good to have Dad coming home again with clay on his clothes, instead of printer's ink. And the smell of clay dust was again in the car. It was a clean, fresh smell, and it meant that Dad was home.

y the mid-1950s, the best of the Ada clay was beginning to run low. They were having to dig deeper, and the quality of it was gradually declining, causing flaws that made more and more pottery unfit for sale. There was an abundance of quality Ada clay on the adjoining property, but the woman who owned the land was now in her advanced years and was unwilling to sell anymore parcels from it. Another clay had to be found. And so my father and his ceramic engineer, Bill Daugherty, launched a state-wide search for an acceptable replacement. One of the first clays to be tested was at Sapulpa being used by the Sapulpa Brick & Tile Company. It fired a redder color, but that was not objectionable. In fact, the redder clay was found to enhance and deepen the dark color variations of all the rutile glazes, as the clay itself contained more iron oxide. There were many ways in which the Sapulpa clay proved superior to the Ada clay. So Sugar Loaf Hill became Frankoma's new clay source.

Another distinct advantage of the Sapulpa clay was that Sugar Loaf was a hill, and clay could be cut in "slices" from the side of it, while Ada clay was dug from a hole in the ground, where rain water and trash often accumulated, making it very difficult in any weather to get to the best quality clay.

Meanwhile, Ada clay was in the mixers, the pipes, hoses, pug mills, and all the many pieces of equipment and machinery used to process and store clay. It would have been far too costly and time consuming to shut the plant down and clean it all out to begin fresh with the Sapulpa clay.

Although the two clays were reasonably compatible, mixing them together produced a different effect than either of them in their pure state. And of course the ratio of one to the other was changing almost daily. So during the several months that it took to change over from Ada clay to pure Sapulpa clay, Bill Dougherty was kept constantly busy adjusting both clay and glaze formulas in order to compensate and bring the ware out as close to the original colors as possible, until the pure Sapulpa clay had could take over the plant.

This may explain some of the slightly—or radically—"off color" pieces from that transitional period that now and then surface and cause us to scratch our heads. I'm sure that if a piece emerged from the kiln that was quite far from being true to color, it might well have been judged as attractive on its own merits and offered for sale anyway, sometimes as a "second," although perfect in every other respect. But these often turn out to be special treasures in our collections, because they're truly "one of a kind."

Many customers during that time who wanted to add to their existing sets, or needed replacement pieces, naturally complained that the color was slightly "off" and didn't really match their other dishes. During that awkward time, Dad shrugged his shoulders a lot, and tried to explain to them what was happening, and persuaded them that the two actually blended well together and made for a unique and interesting table setting. "Look at all the greens out there in nature!" he'd say, pointing out the window. "Do you see any two alike? And does any one clash with the other?" Because my father was such a charmer, almost no one did not buy the story, and almost every customer did purchase those pieces they had come for. But he was also quite right—the two slightly different colors did blend well, and they did make for an interesting table setting. They just needed someone to point it out to them.

CHAPTER 1 2

In the years that followed, service awards began coming from local and state chambers of commerce, as well as many civic clubs throughout a large surrounding area. In his seventh year on the Salvation Army Board of Directors, Dad was elected Chairman, a position in which he was to serve for ten consecutive years. And he was elected President of his beloved Rotary Club.

John Frank and artist
Acee Blue Eagle. c. 1966.

Working closely with the Oklahoma Department of Commerce and Industry, he played a principal role in the establishment of the Made in Oklahoma show that awards outstanding Oklahoma-made products for significant industrial and cultural contributions to community and state. Two years later, Frankoma was the recipient of the Governor's Award for Outstanding Small Business in Oklahoma, and again two years following.

My father was also instrumental in helping develop a ceramics manufacturing program for the Creek Indian Nation. The tribe wanted to produce ceramics commercially, in order to provide more jobs for their people. Dad contributed equipment, materials, and some of his own personnel for many months to teach them the most efficient manufacturing techniques. He also spent much of his own time and energy installing the facility and training the workers.

The Creek Nation repaid my father's service by making him an honorary chief of their tribe, and formalized the honor in a ceremony in which he was crowned with a chief's feathered headdress and given the name "Lumhe Hetke," meaning White Eagle.

But my father's service and generosity took many forms. For him, every day was a new opportunity to go forth in the spirit of giving, and his daily acts proved that he truly believed in sharing the abundance that he had been blessed with.

No matter what the denomination, when John Frank learned that a church was struggling to buy needed equipment, he came to the rescue whenever he could.

There were Baptist, Methodist, Nazarene, Seventh Day Adventist, and Assembly of God churches throughout the area to which he gave air conditioners, hymnals, new pews, carpets, or a small Hammond organ. And many received dozens of plates for their church socials.

Over many years, Frankoma had owned various panel wagons that served as company cars. But they didn't last forever, and about every two or three years they would need replacing. Rather than using them as trade-ins, they were donated to some of the smaller churches and converted to church buses.

1953 Joniece was fifteen. The local school was unfulfilling and provided little challenge for her obvious capabilities. Mother and Dad became aware of her sudden maturity, not only physically and socially, but artistically as well. They observed her restlessness and talked of sending her to a private school that would offer her more opportunity and freedom to grow.

"The price of a private school is just too much!" exclaimed Dad firmly, after some investigation. "It's a luxury we simply can't afford. Maybe next year."

"John," said Mother thoughtfully, "when you need to invest in a piece of equipment for the future of Frankoma, you go to the bank and borrow for it, don't you?"

The point was well taken. "Of course," he said, a bit ashamed.

"If we can invest in labor and machines, do you think an investment in our special child is any less important?"

"Sweetheart, you're right again. It's by far the best investment we could ever make."

"Is there anything left to borrow on?"

Dad thought a moment. "The plant is mortgaged to the hilt. And we promised to leave the house and car debt-free."

Mother smiled. "Well, I guess that's what we've been saving them for, wouldn't you say?"

They embraced as Dad exclaimed happily, "It's settled. Joniece will have the best we can buy!"

Joniece spent three years at Hockaday School in Dallas, and graduated in 1956. And there was no question where she would attend college. She was bound for the University of Oklahoma to study art.

$\mathcal{B}$y 1954, John and Grace Lee had come a long, long way. I was away at college and was engaged to marry soon, Joniece was attending prep school in Dallas, and the time had come to reward themselves. We had lived in many places, all of them makeshift and inadequate. They had longed for a home that was built for the way they wanted to live.

Mother wanted a kitchen that was open to the living area so she would not be separated from family or guests while preparing meals.

For years Dad had talked of a *big* fireplace. "I want one that I can warm something besides my feet!"

There would be enough space so that visiting friends would not be asked to stay at a motel. And there would at last be room to entertain.

It was indeed outlandish and totally impractical, they thought, but Dad really wanted a swimming pool. He at least wanted it to be drawn into the overall plan, so it could be added later when it was more affordable.

The new house would be built as if it were growing out of a hillside. And there would be lots and lots of big trees. And they wanted to incorporate a lot of ceramics and wood for an overall feeling of warmth and earthiness.

Bruce Goff was Professor of Architecture at the University of Oklahoma, and my parents had long admired his magnificent work. His artistic vision had no limits, and he was unafraid to design beyond the bounds of conventional concepts. And Mr. Goff was intrigued and delighted with the unique challenge of designing living space for ceramic artists.

There were many visits to Norman during the following months for conferences with the famous architect. One day my parents returned home as excited and as giddy as two children who had stumbled upon the magic castle. The plans were complete, and they could at last begin to build!

The renderings were taken to the bank for approval of the loan. And to another bank, and to another. To several savings and loans. But the response was consistently the same: "It's, uh . . . certainly interesting. But we're sorry. We can't possibly loan money on anything this, uh . . . unconventional."

Dad and Mother were perplexed by the many rejections. "It feels so right," they pondered. "Can no one see the vision but us?"

One weekend they drove to Bethany to visit Grandpa and Grandma Bowman, as they frequently did. Dad respected the wit and wisdom of my grandfather, and they were as close as if they had been father and son. Their discussions on religion and philosophy and interpretations of the scriptures often went on into the night.

In conversation, Dad told him of the unsuccessful attempts to finance the building of the new home. And Grandpa just laughed smugly.

"Are you praying so the Lord can hear you, John?" he chided as if he were teasing a child.

"Well, Papa, I thought I was. Just what do you mean?"

"You look pretty discouraged to me. And that tells me you're praying only half right."

Dad looked at him blankly and waited for him to elaborate.

"Oh, for heaven's sake, John. Hand me that Bible. Here. You see, in Mark, Chapter 11, it says, 'What things soever ye desire, when ye pray, believe that ye receive them, and ye shall have them.' Now, we know you've been asking. But that's only half of it. Now you've got to go on and know that it's already been taken care of."

Dad covered his eyes in a childish gesture and began to laugh. "Papa, I'm ashamed," he blushed. "I know better. How could I be so stupid! I've been asking and worrying, asking and worrying."

Grandpa's chair went right on rocking as he smiled at my father with profound love. "You'll get your house, John. The Lord already knows what you need. Just get out of His way, and you'll have it before long."

There was much laughing and singing driving back to Sapulpa that night after one of Grandma's wonderful suppers with apple pie and homemade ice cream for dessert.

The following week Dad was asked to speak at a rural Free Methodist Church near Tulsa. The congregation numbered no more than about forty, but he happily accepted as always.

It was an especially warm and receptive group, and after the evening service he had given, coffee and cake were served. Dad was enjoying himself and stayed later than usual to talk and answer questions.

An elderly gentleman with white hair and very casual attire approached Dad and introduced himself, graciously thanking him for taking the time to come and talk to such a small group.

"It's my pleasure, sir," he assured him. "It's not quantity that counts. You surely have a fine group of people here. I can see there's a lot of love working for this church, and I appreciate that."

"Mr. Frank, I hear you're having a hard time securing a loan for your house," he said bluntly. Dad was a bit startled.

"Well—ah—yes, I guess I am. But how did you know?"

The old gentleman chuckled. "As confidential as all that stuff is supposed to be, we bankers still talk under the table, and word gets around. And the word is, nobody'll touch that crazy house of yours! That so?"

Dad agreed, and together they laughed as though the whole idea were folly indeed.

"You're a banker then?"

"Well, not in the strictest sense of the word. You see, I'm president of one of the smaller savings and loan companies in Tulsa. My wife and I like to live out here in the country, though, and we belong to this little church because that's what we're used to. Those great big churches in town are kinda unfriendly, and they don't need my tithe anyway."

Dad was warmed by the candid honesty of the old gentleman.

"They're fools, those big bankers, every one of 'em!" he went on, nudging Dad and slapping his own knee. "How much ya need? Never mind. Just drop by my office sometime this week. Here's my card." And with that, the gentleman rose to leave, and they shook hands.

"The Lord sure works in strange and mysterious ways," Dad mused shaking his head. "I'll bring the plans with me."

"Aw, what in the world for?" the old man laughed. "I'm no architect. Just bring your signature." And he was gone.

"Oh my," said Dad under his breath as he sat back down. "You've done it again, Master, you've done it again. Thank you, Master!"

The Frank home. Sapulpa, Oklahoma, 1957.

*M*other and Dad spent many evenings and weekends thereafter at the plant. There were over two thousand bricks to be glazed and fired. In addition, Bruce Goff and Dad together designed for the entranceway a new and unique "C-Thru" tile, as they called it. The plan required the use of over fifteen hundred of those tiles, and each had to be carefully hand glazed with a brush in four colors.

There were months and months of hard work, but they themselves were creating the materials for the home they would live in. It was hard labor, but a love labor, and in spite of fatigue and aching backs, they pressed and glazed each tile with joy.

And the pottery house shaped like a smile was happily built growing out of a hill among many tall trees. There are three spacious bedrooms, an open kitchen, a very large fireplace, and plenty of space to entertain, inside and out. Oh yes—and a most unique pool stands on the side of that hill as an extension of the living space that John and Grace Lee Frank at last called home.

ABOVE: The fireplace.

RIGHT: The family at home. Christmas, 1962.

all, 1958. My marriage of three years had ended, and I was free to follow my ambition to live in New York City. Soon I found myself standing beside the statue of George M. Cohan at Times Square, feeding the pigeons and watching the Camel man blow smoke rings across Broadway, exactly as I had envisioned when I was nine years old.

Joniece continued to excel in sculpture and all other art media. She earned her degree in art from the University of Oklahoma, where she had studied all the technical courses related to ceramics the school had to offer. It was particularly gratifying for Dad that two of Joniece's textbooks had been authored by his former benefactor at the Chicago Art Institute, Mrs. Myrtle French. Dad's friend and former associate, Professor Joseph Taylor, worked closely with Joniece to help refine her techniques in sculpture and design, and her natural talent as an artist blossomed.

Joniece was twenty-three years old and out of school only a year when she submitted one of her sculptures to the annual Oklahoma Artists Exhibit. Although one of her former teachers had also entered the competition, the jury awarded Joniece first prize.

It was not only an honor to be chosen outstanding artist in the state competition, but it was the first step in establishing herself as a recognized artist, independent of her family. She wanted her works to be judged for whatever they were, not because she was John Frank's daughter. And she had done it!

In the meantime, John and Grace Lee began to travel. They were at last relaxing and enjoying some of the fruits of their labors and struggles during those many long years. They deserved it, and we encouraged them in every way we could to go out and see the world.

There was a trip to Denmark at the invitation of the renowned Royal Copenhagen Potteries. As honored guests, they were treated in every respect as royalty in the world of fine art and craftsmanship.

John Frank (left) with Sir John Wedgwood.
Wedgwood, England, c. 1966.

Years before, Mother had begun collecting the series of Royal Copenhagen Christmas plates. Before their visit had ended, she was presented a gift of the remaining plates that would complete her collection from the first plate dating back to 1908.

There was a month in South America with a Rotary Club group. The following year it was sunny Spain. It was their ambition to see a new country each year to learn what the rest of the world was doing in ceramics, both historic and contemporary.

*J*ohn Frank had always been fascinated with, and always wanted to make, a line of true stoneware products. It was one of his ambitions that never materialized but, true to his nature, he went forward in that direction with every intention to manifest it.

With that in mind, in September of 1958, John Frank bought Synar Ceramics in Muskogee, Oklahoma. Synar had exclusively manufactured artware, flower containers, figurines and such, using a very white clay. He then sent his trusted employee, J. C. Taylor, there to head the operation. According to J. C., the Synar plant actually became very much like a subsidiary, or a second Frankoma Pottery.

Sales-wise, Synar held its own the first year. Dad then decided that it needed a new name. He often referred to the products as the "gray stoneware" (which he hoped it would become) and, when he announced he was looking for an appropriate new name, I suggested a slight shift of the tongue to "Gracetone ware."

The name Gracetone seemed logical to me, and I thought it was rather nice that, in doing so, we could say it had been named for

Mother. Fortunately for us, her name was what it was, and lended itself perfectly. It clicked, and the name was changed.

With the name change came Dad's notion that he would add to Gracetone's line some dinnerware, and he set about designing a new pattern. Dad liked circles. He had always doodled a lot of circles while searching for inspiration, which appeared in many of his designs as far back as the Norman days.

This time he came up with the "circles upon circles" idea and assigned Joniece the task of developing it into a viable pattern and executing all the many pieces in the set, which she did, and it was named "Orbit." He then had Bill Daugherty formulate new glazes for it, and it was offered in Cinnamon Toast and Pink Champagne. The white clay they were using in the Muskogee operation was not suitable for tableware, so he had the red Sapulpa clay hauled down to Muskogee.

There was a time in there that Gracetone and Frankoma were doing a kind of "crossover," and it's often a nightmare for collectors to determine what pieces were made at which plant. And even J. C. himself cannot always distinguish the difference, as they were not very religious about putting a name on the bottom of some of the pieces.

Dad gave samples of the Orbit dinnerware to the Frankoma salesmen to show. But it turned out that, when customers had the choice, Frankoma was almost always chosen over Gracetone. So Orbit never became a real smash hit, no matter how unique and beautiful it was.

However, the Orbit dinnerware was very different in character than anything Frankoma produced, in that all the pieces were very "rounded," with a signature theme of several sizes of circles overlapping each other in a cascading motion, somewhat resembling bubbles or, some say, clouds. To others, it gives the impression of "fantasy," and one romantic collector is positive it represents "the airy daydreams that John and Grace Lee together had dreamed." And she further believes that was the reason he named it Gracetone. Whatever Orbit says to whoever falls in love with it, it can certainly stir the imagination.

The Muskogee operation produced pottery from September of 1958 to May of 1963 and, at its peak, employed as many as thirty people. But there came a time that Dad became disenchanted with the Muskogee plant and closed it. He was always spreading himself too thin and, like many of his other lofty ambitions and intentions, he simply never found the time to bring it to fruition.

J. C. Taylor and his wife bought some of the basic equipment and continued making the established artware line, as well as selling clay and other supplies to hobbyists in the area, and firing their wares for them.

When Dad gave up Gracetone, an agreement was drawn up, giving J. C. exclusive use of the name Gracetone for his pottery as long as he wished. Dad also allowed J. C. to sell Frankoma in the Gracetone showroom on consignment. Whatever Frankoma J. C. sold, he then gave Frankoma the wholesale price. Out of the thousands of wholesale accounts, J. C. was the only one to be given all the Frankoma he wanted, to pay for as it was sold. This way he didn't have to invest any of his own money in stock. My father loved and respected J. C. Taylor far too much to ever question his honesty, and his trust was never betrayed.

After a little more than four years, J. C. and his wife decided to sell their business and move on to something less demanding.

In 1957, Dad made J. C. an offer to return to Frankoma, which he happily accepted. Employees like J. C. didn't come along every day. So the Taylors moved back to Tulsa, and J. C. returned to work at Frankoma.

There was no position in management for J. C. at that time, so he had to start back down the ladder and work his way up again. But in time he was elected secretary of the Frankoma corporation, and became plant supervisor, third in command of plant operations. He continued to fill those positions until December 31, 1985. When he retired, he had worked for Frankoma for a total of forty years.

1960 It was spring, and I had just returned home to New York after completing an exhausting road show when the phone rang. Dad's voice came through the phone in a rush of excitement.

"Surprise, baby! What are your plans for the summer? Would you like to tour Europe with us?"

I had been trying desperately to get hired by any number of summer stock companies that year, and I thought I had heard more "nos" than there were producers. Was this the reason my summer was being kept open for me?

"That's beautiful, Pop!" I gasped. Europe sounded like a dream. "But I really didn't make that much money this last tour, and . . ."

Mother's cheery voice was on the extension. "It's all right, honey, we've already paid for your ticket!"

"Johnnie's coming too, sweetheart, and it's all on the house!" chimed my father, fairly bursting with pride that he could pick up the tab for the entire family. "It's probably the last big trip our family will make together, and we've decided to do it up right. You're with us, aren't you?"

Squeals of laughter were bouncing back and forth on the line when I heard my sister's voice. "Do you think Paris and Rome are ready for two gorgeous single girls like us? We'll devastate 'em!"

My career as an actress/singer at this point left much to be desired, although I managed to work as a temporary secretary between shows to pay for acting school, voice lessons, and the rent on my little sixth-floor Greenwich Village flat (no elevator!). It was going to be such fun to take a rest from pavement pounding and be with my family for two whole months!

The three of them arrived the day before we were to sail, and together we spent the afternoon circling the island of Manhattan on a large excursion boat. The announcer's voice on the loud speaker gave interesting and uninteresting historical facts about the city and pointed out various sites of special interest as we passed.

Shortly after we had craned our necks to see the Brooklyn Bridge as it passed overhead, the voice on the speaker told us that only a few blocks inland was the famous Greenwich Village. "Of course, we all know," he announced with fanfare, "that Greenwich Village is the home of the famous Broadway actress—Donna Frank!"

I froze. Did I hear what I thought I heard? Surely not. I watched the crowded deck of puzzled faces turning to one another asking, "Who?"

Just then I spotted Dad leaning over the rail, overacting with mock interest and stretching himself for a glimpse of the famous landmark. He continued his performance until he caught my eye and ran to me with a hug, laughing mischievously at his own game.

"You're famous, baby! Now *everybody* knows your name!"

My father had tipped the announcer ten dollars to read over the loud speaker the script he had written for him on the back of an ice cream wrapper.

*T*he travel posters claimed, "Half the fun is getting there!" And they were right. The week on the boat introduced us to scores of people from many countries whom we would never have met otherwise.

We first discovered England. Then France, Germany, Austria, Holland, Switzerland, Italy, and Greece. It was a small group in which we traveled. In addition to our family, there were only four, plus our guide, Dr. Donald Humphrey, Director of Tulsa's Philbrook Art Center.

Dr. Humphrey had conducted tours like this for many years and was well traveled in Europe. Soon Johnnie and I were calling him Don, and he became our best pal. During the daytime, we were shown every museum and statue to be seen. However, many evenings around 9:30, Johnnie and I watched the others collapse into their rooms for the night, while we waited up for a familiar knock at our door.

Don was our trusted escort, and he delighted in taking my sister and me on royal tours of the London, Paris, Rome, Vienna, and Athens that American tourists still may never know.

It was a summer to remember forever. My parents were always the very best and most pleasurable companions with whom we could have traveled. We rode on trains, hopped planes, and were jostled in the backs of broken-down old buses, while we ate funny breads and tried new kinds of smelly cheeses. We invented stories about the Greek gods, threw coins in all the fountains, and renamed equestrian statues throughout Europe.

It was an important and significant vacation for our family. We were never to forget the extraordinary historical sites we visited together and the sights we shared; the many things we found to laugh about, as well as those things we found beautiful enough to cry about; and the outrageous stories we invented to fill those gaps in history that for us needed an explanation.

But Dad was right. It was the last vacation our family would take together. And the closeness we experienced as a family will never be forgotten and can never be repeated.

CHAPTER 14

*M*any famous European ceramic institutions evolved from a century or two of experience in the refinement of materials and design, and their names have long been synonymous with quality and tradition.

John Frank, however, had no such romantic history or tradition behind him. He was an upstart maverick in the world's ceramic industry. He chose his particular profession because it was the best way he knew to love and serve all of mankind—to give them beauty they could bring into their homes and live with as a daily reminder that they, too, can become clay in the Master's hands and become a vessel of service and beauty. It was the universal message that he wanted to present to all people everywhere, and being a potter was the way in which he chose to "pass it on."

He also aspired to do something no American potter had yet done. He wanted to create a series of fine plates that would depict the real meaning of Christmas. So in 1965 the first annual Christmas plate made in America came into being. Once again John Frank started a trend in American ceramics. It was to be a limit edition series, and the mold would be destroyed at a special ceremony each Christmas Eve.

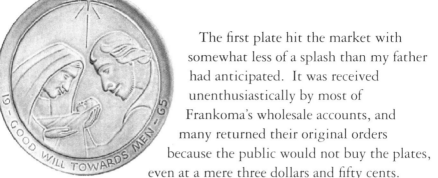

First Frankoma
Christmas plate. 1965.

The first plate hit the market with somewhat less of a splash than my father had anticipated. It was received unenthusiastically by most of Frankoma's wholesale accounts, and many returned their original orders because the public would not buy the plates, even at a mere three dollars and fifty cents. Other dealers marked the plates down to half price, just to move them out of their stores.

Sales of the 1966 Christmas plate were no more successful than the first. And neither was the third in 1967. Dad was bewildered. Where had he gone wrong? When the idea had come for the creation of the series, he had obeyed his feelings and gone forward with dedication and enthusiasm, believing with all his heart that it had been an inspiration from the Master. But if the Master had directed him to design this series of Christmas plates, why had it failed? They simply were not selling as they should. Should he abandon the idea and discontinue manufacturing them altogether?

He began to look more carefully at what he had done and examine those feelings that had motivated him to launch such an ambitious work. There was a missing piece that kept the pattern of success from being complete. What was it, and where would he look for it?

Dad was not displeased with what he had created. In fact, he was rather proud of those three plates. He liked them. So, despite the uncertainty that plagued him for those three years, he firmly resolved to go ahead and design a fourth Christmas plate, if only to please himself. It made him feel good. Whether the series had a future or not, he wanted to do another. "Let's give it one more try," he said. "If I can do something even better this year, it just might catch on."

*Y*outh for Christ in Tulsa was housed in one small, run-down office when John Frank first discovered it in 1968. It was decidedly unimpressive, and he exclaimed to Dave Cox, then managing director, "No wonder your membership is so low! I wouldn't want to belong to a group that can't do better than this for a headquarters!"

He learned that the membership of young people numbered only about thirty in the Tulsa chapter. "What a disgrace! The Master said we should have abundance. So let's get busy and do something about all this. If we're going to talk about Him to young people, first we've got to practice what we're preaching!"

In the face of what was, my father's positive words brought him an instant invitation to the next Board of Directors meeting, which had already been called for the express purpose of disbanding the Tulsa chapter of YFC. And my father entered that meeting with the immutable faith that he had been chosen for this specific task requiring his unique energies, again to serve the youth, and he joyfully accepted the assignment. As always, he would go all the way, full speed ahead.

His first job was to convince the existing board members that YFC must not only be revived, but that it could rise to new levels of effectiveness. He felt with all his heart that the work of introducing Christian living principles to young people was imperative, and the responsibility of keeping that work alive lay with the small group of businessmen in that very room.

His insistence that day that they individually and collectively accept the challenge given them by the Master inspired new dedication in those present, and he walked away from the meeting the newly elected chairman.

Dad knew many gentlemen in the Tulsa area who called themselves Christians. He pondered for days and prayed to be shown which branches would bear the best fruit. He then sat down and carefully made a list of those with whom he was personally acquainted and knew to be enjoying financial abundance in their lives. In a few days he had called on each of them in person. Soon there was money to work with.

With the newly collected contributions (including a sizeable sum from his own pocket) Dad, working with Dave Cox, began the reorganization by designing a campaign to energize the Tulsa chapter of Youth for Christ.

Dave Cox and Dad deeply respected each other and shared a sincere dedication to an important work. It was an effective team. YFC membership began to climb. Dad traveled to many campuses and gave his famous talk about being clay in the Master's hands. Many young college students heard the message and volunteered to work to spread the good news of a new, exciting, and fruitful life.

YFC was at last an entity that its members could point to with pride. It was working! Soon Dad's ambition for the chapter took another leap forward, and he began looking for a plot of ground on which to build a new YFC headquarters in Tulsa.

Architect Bruce Goff was personally commissioned by John Frank to draw up plans for the new center. Nothing ordinary here would do. It would be a building unique in all the world of course, as all of Goff's buildings are. And of course Dad would create a special Frankoma tile to be incorporate throughout the structure. Nothing was too good for YFC. It would be nothing short of magnificent!

YFC was his baby. He had found it when it was down and out. "It must be done! If I don't do it, who will?"

Many discouraging and seemingly insurmountable difficulties arose for Youth for Christ, but my father never looked at them as problems. Others stood by and said, "How will we ever do it?" But he never once admitted an obstacle could not be overcome; rather he would laugh, clap his hands, and shout, "Let's do it, boys!" And regardless of the problem, whether it was acquiring necessary equipment, meeting tough deadlines, bridging communication barriers, or a general lack of money—nothing disturbed the peace and abiding faith in which he lived. It surrounded him like an aura.

When there was no answer in sight, Dad merely found a place where he could be alone and asked for one. He would then go forward, knowing that the solution was just around the next corner. And it always was. "If the Master gives you an assignment, you can be sure He's going to give you all the help you need to get the job done!"

My father learned from the painful lessons of his past and made sure he did not repeat the mistakes he had made with The American Patriot. He claimed that he had confidently known at every turn the right path to take for the good of Youth for Christ. He ultimately recognized that the old American Patriot trauma had been given him in preparation for the revitalization of this important movement.

My father's remarkably effective leadership in Youth for Christ was truly a testament to the truth that God works in strange and mysterious ways—but He does work. When we find ourselves in a situation that causes us pain, it is in ignorance that we judge it as "bad." But if we become fully conscious that it has been given to strengthen us for challenges yet to come, it becomes far less difficult to approach it as a "lesson" and do it with pleasure, rather than with dread and fear.

My father adopted this universal law as part of his personal philosophy and lived it daily. There were no unpleasant tasks, nor was there an unimportant one. To him, they were all the same. Each was but another exercise, another opportunity to love and serve. And that's the way he met each day's work.

"What else is there to do while we're here?" he'd laugh with a shrug. "We always have a choice—to love it, or to dread it and waste our energy complaining about it. I chose a long time ago to go forward and love it all—because that's what makes me feel good. Once you know you have that choice, it's easy."

Dad was driving home from Tulsa one afternoon, when he spotted what he thought was just the right piece of property for the new YFC building. But on investigation he learned that it was almost hopelessly tied up in litigation. However, he felt so strongly about the suitability of the location, he would not be discouraged.

Several months passed. Scores of meetings and hundreds of phone calls later, and finally, the land title was presented to Youth for Christ. Construction of the new headquarters was soon to be under way.

Bruce Goff's first design was submitted to Dad for approval. He looked it over and studied it carefully. But there were no fireworks—no bells rang for him. He returned the renderings and told Bruce that it wasn't what he had in mind. Anyone else would have been reluctant to tell one of the world's leading architects that what he had designed simply wasn't grand enough. But John Frank didn't know that, so he did it anyway. He made some sweeping suggestions and told him to go back to the drawing board and try again.

An architect's time is expensive, and this one was certainly no different. Bruce's work was in great demand, and his time was not plentiful. But it didn't matter to Dad. He wanted the new center to be nothing short of extraordinary and simply wouldn't settle for anything less. So time went by, and design costs continued to rise. The second and third designs were submitted, and they were all very nice, but Bruce's ideas still did not match the vision in Dad's mind. It never occurred to him that time was a factor. To him there was all the time in the world, and whatever time it took, it would be done right. And so time passed.

The Youth for Christ board met one morning in hopes of finding a solution to the problem of the organization's inadequate cash flow. Dave Cox had given a report of its income vs. expenses, and all had left the meeting glum and discouraged.

After the meeting adjourned, Dad and Dave walked into a small local cafe and seated themselves at a table near the window. They both sat in silence for a long time. While they waited for their lunch to be served, Dad stirred his coffee thoughtfully.

His gaze soon fixed upon a small chip on the handle of the cup. Hmm. A missing piece. A missing piece that did not hamper in any way the cup's purpose or its performance.

He lifted the cup and examined its base. Another even larger chunk of the cup was missing from the bottom, yet both flaws were virtually unnoticeable.

Closing his eyes, a broad confident smile made his face light up, and he began to chuckle. "Dave, my boy, I've got it!" he whispered. "I think I've got it!"

Upon leaving the restaurant, the two men drove directly to the attorney's office. An agreement was drawn up whereby Youth for Christ would receive a percentage of all profits that were realized from the sale of the Frankoma Christmas plates.

Suddenly the American public began to realize the collectability of the series and hurried out to buy them in quantity.

Sales of the 1968 Christmas plate rose steadily, as did the 1969. People were scrambling for the previous 1965 issue, and its cash value began to rise. Antique dealers were suddenly buying each new issue in quantity and hoarding them for the day their value would mature into healthy profits.

It was as if the dam had broken; what had once been a trickle became a veritable flood. The first American annual Christmas plate began appearing in antique magazines and collectors' listings all over the world. Outrageous prices were asked—and outrageous prices were paid—for the 1965 plate.

Many books and periodicals being published on the subject of collectibles, valuable ceramics, antiques, or fine china, included a feature on the soon-to-be-rare limited edition plates being created by a Southwestern artist named John Frank. Thousands of letters poured into the office, and people called from all across the country to ask if there were anymore 1965 plates available at any price.

You see, the success of the plate did not require that my father alter the Christmas story in any way. The only thing that changed was the manner in which the profits were channeled.

My father steadfastly believed that the Master conducts His work in this world through each of us. When we ask Him to make us His tool, He'll show us clearly what He wishes us to do. And the work is assigned to each of us according to our individual talents. Dad recognized that God was using him to serve His people in the same way a potter uses clay to create objects of service. So Dad likewise used clay to illustrate how easy it is to allow the Master to mold us into objects of service to humankind.

CHAPTER 15

In the inevitable drama of time, Dad's tremendous stamina began to wane. He was sixty-six years old, and his pace had not slowed from the time he was a young man. And now his body was giving him messages he did not wish to acknowledge.

"It never once occurred to me that I'd ever get old. Is that what's happening to me? Am I getting old?"

"Papa, you could never be old. You've taken good care of your body, but you've also demanded a lot of it. Now you must treat it more kindly than ever. Try to rest, Papa."

He was furious! The very thought of refusing those who asked him to speak was embarrassing and painful. What could he say—"Sorry, I can't go on doing it all—I'm not young anymore"? It was too humiliating.

Death did not frighten my father. Becoming old did. What would happen to all the things he had started? What if he had to discontinue certain projects before he could see them completed? What would happen to YFC?

When he needed help, he had always asked. But this time it was different. It seemed foolish and unreasonable to ask for more youthful energy to carry on. Could he ask, then truly believe the old stamina he once had would be returned to him? Was it a fair request?

For several days my father stayed to himself and wrestled with his anxieties and frustrations. He prayed and meditated for long hours trying to calm his fears and uncertainties.

When our family gathered that Christmas, 1969, we all became distressingly aware that Papa was not well, and shortly thereafter we persuaded him to enter the hospital for a complete and thorough physical examination.

The tests were to take several days, during which time scores of friends, associates, and various clergy and coworkers in the community and surrounding areas came to visit and wish him well.

One evening when several of his closest friends were present, the telephone beside his bed rang. Papa answered with a hearty, "Hello, hello!" He began to listen intently, and soon he covered his face and said, "Thank you. Thank you so much. Oh my. What honor you do me! Thank you."

He sat up in bed and began to compose himself. One of the gentlemen stepped forward and took the phone. When he spoke, we realized that he was there for that purpose, knowing the call would come.

Papa finished his thank yous and hung up the phone with a humble smile. "Tell them, Tom," he said. "You tell them."

Tom spoke as proudly as if he were announcing the President of the United States. "John has just been given a very special service award by the World Conference of Youth for Christ for his unselfish contributions and outstanding leadership. Dave Cox has just accepted the award for him in Atlanta, Georgia. John, we're so grateful to you. You've been such an example to all of us. We've learned so much from you about living!"

Papa was deeply moved, as we all were, and we crowded around him, laughing and hugging him with congratulations.

Youth for Christ, for which he had served two years on the International Board of Directors, had run a close second in his heart to his own Frankoma Pottery. He had devotedly poured his energies into it because it was important to him that youth be pointed in the right direction, and encouraged to live according to Christian life principles.

When the work of putting YFC into the operating black had been sloughed off by others as impossible, my father had accepted the responsibility personally, having received his instructions to get out there and find a way. And young men and women from all over the world were saying thank you.

*T*he day arrived that Papa was to be released by his doctors, and the four of us gathered to hear the word that no one is ever prepared to hear.

The doctor explained, "Of the many, many known forms of cancer, Mr. Frank, you're fortunate in this respect—we can treat prostate cancer. We can almost certainly retard its growth for an indefinite period of time." He smiled with effort and added, "You needn't consider yourself a terminal patient. Be assured that we don't."

Nevertheless, when the man in white had departed, the four of us sat stunned, unable to move. Not a word was spoken until Papa stood and motioned us to him. We made a close circle with our arms around each other, and Papa began to speak.

"Thank you, Father, for bringing together those I love most to be with me today." His voice wavered, and minutes went by as he struggled to continue.

"There's so much to be done, Master—and I'm asking Your permission to finish what I've started. I place myself in Your loving hands, Master, and whether or not this request is granted—above all, Thy will be done."

"Thy will be done," we repeated together in affirmation.

When my father returned to work in his studio, it was with a new urgency that was troubling to those who worked closely with him. There was no longer the natural flow of energy that had long made him move with grace and ease. His movements were now forced, motivated by a feverish determination to win against the enemy Time.

Papa deliberately flooded his schedule and began designing more furiously than ever. As he demanded more of himself, he also demanded more of his staff.

He pushed even Joniece to new limits. His irritability grew in those months, and no one could slow him down long enough to remind him of the adverse consequences to his health. If he were to be allowed the time to finish what he had begun, he would not be guilty of wasting an hour of it!

1970 The Christmas plate was nearing completion when Papa became dissatisfied with what he had created. An entirely new concept had come to him. Destroying the old, he resolutely began again.

To now, Papa had wisely accepted Grace Lee's criticism and advice in all his work, as her suggestions had never failed to be valuable. However, this time he spoke to no one, and any assistance offered was ignored or irritably refused. His mind was rigidly set. The 1970 plate would offer a standing Christ child, backed by a large cross—alpha and omega—birth and death in one bold motion.

The design of this particular plate was far more labored than all the others. The creation of it consumed him day and night. Time after time he tore it down and began again. It was as if he had been commanded by the Master Himself to make a pictorial statement concerning the truth about life and death. He was near exhaustion as the production deadline approached.

At long last it was finished. He proudly unveiled it to family and staff, then stepped back in anticipation of their usual approving comments. He was not disappointed. Although no one fully understood its meaning, all had watched him endure the labor pains suffered to give it birth, and could not bring themselves to offer less than the highest praise.

When they saw the figure of the baby Jesus, it was apparent what the major struggle had been. It was the child's face. Dad had wanted so desperately to portray the innocence of an infant, as well as the wisdom of a loving Messiah. The hands and arms were those of a newborn babe, outstretched in loving invitation; the swaddling clothes were soft and well wrapped around the child's body; the cross in the background was bold and foreboding; and the letters at the bottom plainly hailed His identity—KING OF KINGS.

But there was the child's face. Not at all the face of a child, but that of an old man. My father had unconsciously given the child his own face. No one dared say it, and he was never aware he had fashioned an unmistakable self portrait.

The 1970 Christmas plate was to be the least popular of the series because it lacked the traditional aesthetic beauty of the others, but it was nevertheless the statement my father wished to make. Even I did not question it when I saw it for the first time at the holidays. Neither would I risk offending him.

"Johnnie, do you think he knows?"

"He's too close to it. He doesn't see."

"Are others aware of what he has done?"

"A few perhaps," she replied. "But I can't help feeling that if the public ever realizes what this particular plate represents, and what it meant to him, it could turn out to be the most valuable of the series."

*P*apa once again became cheerful and easy as soon as his plate was in production. He continued to complete his various projects, one by one, although he slowly resigned himself to a schedule that included less work and more rest.

However, it would be untrue to say that he became his "old self" in the months that followed. The chemotherapy treatments for his illness were anything but easy for him, and his body was to undergo many radical and disturbing changes. The cancer was spreading to other parts of his body. Nevertheless, he continued in the faith that his pain and discomfort were for him to experience and accept, without questioning God's reason for asking him to bear it.

$\mathcal{M}$ ike Bordon of the Oklahoma Small Business Administration had prepared a large dossier on my father which included his history of personal achievements, community service, and contributions to state commerce, supplemented with scores of stories and letters from people who had known him and served with him since he came to Oklahoma in 1927, until 1971. The impressive testimonial to John Frank's life took Mr. Bordon a full year to compile and assemble.

It was then submitted to the SBA, and my father was nominated for Outstanding Small Businessman of the Year in the State of Oklahoma. The candidates for the title were unaware that they were in competition until the final decision was made.

When it was announced that John Frank had been chosen Oklahoma's Outstanding Small Businessman, it was a surprise. And yet no one was surprised at all. He had earned it, of course.

The same book that won for him the state title was then sent to Washington, D.C., where the winners from each state assembled for the national title. This time it was no surprise at all when the title of Outstanding Small Businessman in America was awarded to my father.

Our entire family made the trip to Washington to watch him accept this prestigious award. Senators, representatives, and national SBA officials treated us royally when we arrived at the Capitol.

When he was introduced, he approached the podium, and every person in the plush banquet hall rose to their feet to applaud him. They continued to cheer as he stood before them and looked humbly into their faces. When all were seated at last, he was silent for a long while before he was able to speak.

"This is something one doesn't run for, you know," he began, choking back the emotion. "And that's why this is such an honor." Every person watching him knew well those feelings and waited in empathy as he tried to speak the words that were reluctant to come forth. He wiped his eyes and cleared his throat. "Thank you, Mike Bordon, for believing in the first place that I was worthy of this honor."

Introducing Mother, he said, "Grace Lee has always been my partner, and this is as much her award as it is mine. My two daughters, Joniece and Donna, have been my greatest supporters. My family is the most important asset to my life."

My father related how Frankoma began and spoke of the many times he could have been discouraged enough to quit and walk away.

"I soon learned that worry kills, work doesn't. So I refuse to worry! You see, I can hire people do that for me." Each businessman in the room related the statement to their own lives and their applause confirmed their agreement.

"Most people don't like to talk about religion or politics. But they're both important to me, and I talk about them every chance I get. I'm not embarrassed to stand up before everyone and say that I'm here because I love my God and I love to serve Him."

Papa was relaxing now and beginning to talk to these people in the same friendly and personal manner that he had shown a thousand other audiences. These outstanding men knew they were not hearing just another dry acceptance speech, and they listened intently.

"Frankoma is unique. We don't make anything people have to have. We make something they have to want. So that's why it's even more remarkable that I'm standing here before you today. Yes, I'm a businessman—but first of all, I'm an artist who creates things people want to live with.

"Art is not art if it doesn't make a statement. So you see, if one of the items we make doesn't sell well enough to remain in the line for at least ten years, we haven't said anything.

"My aim has never been to become a wealthy man. To gain money for me is to spend it. I have a few good suits and a nice convertible car, but I don't get a new one every year—I wear it out. I found a long time ago that people are a better investment. And when I was a young man, I told the Master that, above all else in this life, I wanted to serve Him by serving His people. And He's been so good to me. I've had everything in life and so much more than I ever thought I wanted! And now this honor today."

There was another long and eloquent silence. "I'm so grateful. I thank all of you who chose me as America's Outstanding Small Businessman. And I appreciate each of you who came to share with me the joy of receiving this great honor."

The audience again stood and applauded him, shouting "Bravo!" as flash bulbs popped from all directions. Mr. Kleppe, Administrator of the National Small Business Administration, stood at the podium and asked, "Mrs. Frank, since your husband insists that you're also the recipient of this award, would you please come forward?"

Mother stepped to the podium with a radiant smile. "It's true we've been a team. I knew the day I met him that together we could do anything in the world we set out to do. And if I had searched a lifetime, I couldn't have found a better father for my two daughters."

Her speech was appropriately brief, but it was very much in harmony with the sentiment shared by each of the nation's outstanding businessmen and their wives.

*T*he following morning I prepared to fly to Ohio where I had been contracted to sing the lead in a historical drama staged in a large new amphitheater near Dover. Rehearsals were to begin the following day.

The rest of my family was about to board the limousine that would take them to the White House when one of the security men stopped my mother and sister from entering.

"I'm sorry, Mr. Frank, our orders are to present only you to the President. Your family will remain here."

Papa stood tall and without hesitation replied, "Then please give my regrets to the President and say that I cannot come today."

There was a brief moment of silence before the man cleared his throat and managed to say, "I beg your pardon, sir?"

Papa smiled confidently. "You see, two of the most important reasons that the President is seeing me today are standing there beside you. It wouldn't make much sense if I were to go without them, now would it?"

"But, Mr. Frank, they've not been cleared through security—and that would take some time. I'm sure you understand."

Papa nodded politely. "Yes, I understand. We'll wait."

Without a word, the manicured man stepped into the limousine and closed the door. He picked up the telephone and talked very rapidly for what must have been ten minutes or more. When he emerged from the car, he soberly opened the rear door and motioned for all three to enter.

The sleek black vehicle moved swiftly towards the mansion on Pennsylvania Avenue. Papa held his head high and wore the pleased smile of a winner.

Once inside the impressive residence, there was another considerable delay while two unexpected guests were rushed through security clearance. A bevy of badged officials scurried about in a maze of papers and rubber stamps and governmental red tape that evolved at last into one gracious smile and the words, "The President will see you now."

Mr. Nixon received them with sincere warmth and interest. He patiently posed with them for White House photographers, while he and my father chatted as comfortably as old friends.

In the three days of luncheons, dinners, and parties to celebrate and congratulate, it was all said. John Frank was an example of how life serves you when first you choose to serve.

Left to right: John Frank, President Richard M. Nixon, Grace Lee, Joniece, and Thomas Kleppe, Director of the U.S. Small Business Administration. Washington, D.C., 1971. John Frank is named "Outstanding Small Businessman in America."

CHAPTER 16

*M*y father went about methodically finishing most of the projects he had begun, not only at Frankoma, but also those community and statewide projects involving civic organizations in which he had been involved. Where he had served on a continuing basis, he replaced himself with persons whom he felt were capable of carrying on in his stead.

For six years he had served on the Board of Directors of the Sapulpa library. He had gone to great lengths to help obtain funds from state and federal sources, as well as from local organizations and individuals. In addition, he persuaded one of the town's affluent citizens to match whatever monies could be raised for the library's expansion, thus doubling the fund and putting it over its goal.

He was determined to see the completion of the new $225,000 library wing, and he did. Because of the dedication and the energy he devoted to the expansion, the new auditorium would bear the name of Frank Hall.

On the other hand, John Frank's dreams for Youth for Christ had been too big, too expensive, and his time had run out. If he could have lived long enough to see it built, he would surely have found a way to pay for it. But plans ground to an unfortunate halt when he was forced to resign because of his failing health.

Youth for Christ sold the land my father had acquired for them and bought a former church building near the University of Tulsa, which they named the John Frank Center. But without him, the energy that had supported and propelled the organization forward rapidly waned. The entity would maintain itself for a time, but not with the same drive and vision. The chapter ultimately dissolved.

I had moved to Los Angeles in 1957 for a year, moved to New York City for six years, then returned to LA in 1964. I left for brief periods to accept work (theatrical and nontheatrical) in other

John and Grace Lee Frank. November, 1971.

states. But LA always felt like home, and I just kept returning. So I finally took root and made my home where I was the most content, and there I had remained.

For two long years, my father's face had grown pale and his body had lost more of its strength and firmness. And so it was in the summer of 1973 that Papa returned to Tulsa's St. Francis Hospital for more tests and treatments. In California, I began to feel an unnameable need to be with him, and time only increased the sense of urgency. I didn't question those feelings, as I had learned long ago that they were messages. Rather than deny them and make excuses to the contrary, I called the airlines.

Cheerfulness filled the hospital room as I ran to greet him. We hugged each other as always like two playful bears, and I fought back my tears when I saw how thin he had become. I was struck with the reality of what his debilitating illness had done to him.

After our greetings, I excused myself to go "freshen up" and hurried down the hall to the lounge.

"They're killing him," I thought. "They're supposed to be curing him, and they're killing him!" I was still in shock from the sight of his face. I felt a tremendous compassion for both Mother and Joniece, and I couldn't hold back the tears.

"They're going through the same ordeal," I thought. "But they're here dealing with it daily. I live half a nation away, so I just get a series of shocks with rests in between." I tried hard to reason and understand it from an honest and unemotional perspective. "I suppose it's given to each of us in the way that we can best deal with it."

Then I considered Papa himself. "He knows, of course. And he's handling it better than the three of us put together." I closed my eyes and tried to calm my welling feelings of anger and helplessness before returning to his room.

In the excitement of seeing Papa, I hadn't noticed that his room was not the usual private one. While I had been gone, the gentleman who occupied the other bed had returned.

Papa's introduction of Mr. Sullivan told me that they had become quite close friends in the few days they had shared the room. The man was several years younger than Papa. He was tall, with strong features, and his enthusiastic smile poured a positive warmth into the room. His wife had come to take him home.

I was told that these good people were neighbors of mine, residents of Santa Monica, California. Mr. Sullivan, while visiting their children in Tulsa, had suffered a mild heart attack. They would be a few more days with their family and then return to California.

Mr. Sullivan and Papa had been the very best of company for each other and had exchanged many stories that provided each other with strength. They had prayed together daily, and a very strong bond had evolved, because their dedication and faith were of equal intensities. What joy to see Papa in such good spirits!

What luck that there had been no private rooms available in order to bring these two men together for mutual support! But of course it had not been luck at all. It seems when the heart is right, we are given what is needed, and always at the right time. We are never abandoned. It was suddenly very obvious to me that Papa was more together and far more comfortable with this than any of us.

At that moment, I realized that all was as it was meant to be, and I vowed not to interfere by trying to hold on and resist the inevitable.

Mom and I spent most of the next day, Saturday, with Papa, while Joniece doubled her duties at the plant in his absence. She arrived from work at dinnertime, and the three of us left together for the cafeteria. Mom had become so depressed we had to coax her to eat.

I wanted so very much to be of some comfort to my mother and my sister at that time. I wished they could accept that the situation would not change for the better, but rather see that the change had to be in our eyes, in the way we were looking at what was happening. It was all evolving perfectly—according to another Plan, not ours—and we could not influence the course of it one way or the other. However, we could surely make it infinitely more bearable for Papa, and for ourselves, if we could only alter our understanding of it.

I was of course unsuccessful in my attempts and felt from them a subtle resentment toward what they perceived as irreverent, even sacrilegious, in my efforts to understand such an overwhelmingly defeating thing as Papa's illness and (we had not yet said the word) death. So I let it go and said no more about it.

The next day was Sunday, and Papa told the nurses to "barricade the door!" because we positively did not want to see anyone. The doctors were to release him to go home the next morning, and I would fly back to Los Angeles. It was our day to be alone together, and his spirits were high.

Printing a big DO NOT DISTURB sign bordered with flowers, he taped it to the door and playfully jumped back in bed.

"Now! Tell me everything!"

After some light conversation about how I loved living in Marina del Rey, goings on at Frankoma, and more chitchat about relatives and friends, we began to talk more seriously.

I told my father that I wanted to get out of show business once and for all—I didn't need it anymore, and it certainly didn't need me. I had worked as an assistant to a chiropractic physician in Hollywood, and it had led me to the study of many alternative kinds of healing, including the field of metaphysical phenomena related to healing. And that in turn had compelled me to investigate various states of human consciousness known for centuries to the American Indian. I now felt more than ever that I wanted to be involved in some way in the field of healing, but I didn't know how. I just knew I was being pulled in that direction.

"Drugs and surgery can't be the only answer, Papa. China and Tibet have successfully treated all kinds of human illnesses for thousands of years with techniques Western doctors refuse to even take a look at! Why?

"Even the Indian medicine man often had a better rate of cure than we do today, and I'm learning about all kinds of alternative healing methods that work with a lot less pain, without side effects, and faster recuperation periods.

"Papa, I began seriously focusing on American Indian cultures over a year ago. I wanted to know why they were considered at one time, in their purest state, the most spiritually advanced race on the planet."

"Oh? And what did you find?"

"Well, I learned a whole lot of things. I don't know where to begin," I replied uncertainly. "I've learned a lot about their 'religion,' if you can call it that. It wasn't a religion, though, as we think of a religion. It was simply the way they thought and lived and knew things to always be. Their lives were their religion. Kind of like the way you don't separate your life and your religion. Religion isn't something you have, but something you know and are.

"For you, the church is a place where people can come together and share their stories and learn how to make what the Master taught work for them—not a place to stand and sing songs with the same enthusiasm you'd read a grocery list."

Dad laughed loudly and slapped his knee. "I know what you're talking about, baby. I know what you're saying!"

"Why don't people live what they say they believe? Why do they go to all the trouble to decorate themselves and go to church on Sunday morning, when they know that by Monday they'll be right back to being their old profane selves? What in the world can they be thinking about?"

Papa looked at me long and lovingly. "It's good to hear you saying these things, honey. It means you've lived enough to take a mirror to yourself and start asking the right questions."

"Well, that's what I'm coming to, Pop—I've been asking a lot of questions, and I'm finally getting some answers. I've been looking at myself good and hard—and I'm seeing I'm not really who I thought I was all this time."

He was fairly beaming. I knew he understood perfectly, but he said nothing. I tried hard not to, but I could feel the tears coming.

"Come and sit over here by me," he said. "Tell me more."

I sat on the edge of his bed, and he held my hand.

"The Indians taught me so much, Papa—not a lot of information, but they taught me by their example. Each time I go back and read the words of the great Chiefs, I see that my life is nothing more than a cop-out. I gotta do something about myself, Papa. It feels like my life is just one big lie!"

He stroked my hair the way he did when I was a child and hurting. "The Spirit is always there, baby. But in order for us to have the experience, we have to be ready and open and wanting it. We can try to help others get tuned in to it, but in the end we're only responsible for our own awareness of it.

"So when others around you are there because it's the social thing to do, or whatever, it mustn't upset you. If it does, you're only keeping yourself from experiencing all that you came there to experience. The Holy Spirit is a very intimate and personal thing, you know."

He took me by the shoulders and looked into my eyes. "If we do not know God, it's not His fault. God always stands waiting for us to become ready and willing and longing to know Him intimately."

"I know. I do know." I dried my eyes. "A few months ago I had an opportunity to go to Arizona with an Indian friend of mine to take part in one of their healing ceremonies. And I did."

My father's face lit up with an approving smile. "How wonderful! I've always wondered about that. Tell me! What was it like?"

"I was shown how to lift my consciousness and open myself to the Great Spirit and . . . well, they showed me how to open my 'inner eyes' wide, Papa, so that everything I looked at I saw in a totally different way than ever before. It's like all the things around me—animate and inanimate—sort of took on a life and a consciousness of its own and loved me and told me things I never knew before."

He didn't fully understand, and I didn't expect him to. But he knew that what I had experienced was a positively wonderful thing, and he smiled to urge me on.

"It was my *understanding* that received a healing, Papa! They showed me how it's all put together. The whole world is so exquisitely designed that everything in it is linked together to all make up one thing. I mean I actually saw it all as the One. Nothing is separate! It's that First Commandment—'Thou shalt love the One.'"

Our conversation had been so intense, we were startled when a crisply starched nurse waltzed into the room with a little paper cup of pills on a tray.

"Don't forget where we were," he whispered behind his hand. "Now, what's this one for—to wake me up or put me to sleep? I don't need either one, so go away!" he commanded, giving the nurse a wink.

"Mr. Frank, doctor's orders are . . ."

"I don't need a doctor today. And next time, read the sign!"

The nurse pursed her lips without humor, wrote something on her clipboard, and left the room as abruptly as she had entered.

"They'll drive me crazy with pills! Now, where were we . . ."

"How everything is all connected," I resumed. "You know your body is made up of billions of cells, all holding together to make up one whole unit called a body."

"That I can understand. Go on . . ."

"You must understand, of course, that 'you' are not your body, or your feelings or your thoughts or your personality, none of those things. Those are just physical things that the real 'you' is living in and with for right now so it can move around on the Earth plane and express itself, okay?"

"Right on!" he exclaimed, not minding in the least to use my jargon.

"What 'you' are is a single cell of consciousness—pure awareness—that happens to be living in this body for a while."

"Gotcha!"

"So each living soul on this planet—no, in all the universes in all of space everywhere—is also one cell of pure consciousness. Are you with me?"

"I'm with ya, baby!" he laughed.

"And the same way in which those physical cells all cling together to make one body, we 'consciousness cells' all exist together to make up one . . ." I didn't know the word. The closest I could come to it was, "thought."

We were silent for a moment. Then Papa pointed his finger and exclaimed, "Idea! It's like a giant idea that we make!"

"Okay, I'll buy that. At least we're on the same frequency."

"Wait! I've got it!" He covered his face like a child playing hide and seek. We were now laughing like two cosmic children, excited at having found a new game. "Is that like . . ."

I anticipated his question. "Yes, that's the same principle and process of cloning. Every single cell has in it the blueprint of the entire entity. All the information is in every cell, so that each cell has the potential of becoming another entire unit identical to the one it's a part of."

"Now I see what it means when a person says, 'I am God.' I've always been offended at that—it seems like such an awfully egotistical and blasphemous thing to say."

"No more egotistical than if one of your cells were to jump up and say, 'I'm John Frank!' Because potentially it is, and with the right direction and catalyst it would be."

"Sure!" he whispered almost reverently. "When you understand it like that . . ."

I led him on. "And where does this giant 'idea,' the one we're each a cell of, live—if you were to go looking for it?"

Now Papa was wiping his eyes, half crying, half laughing. "Naturally. God is in the space all around us and through us. My, what a revelation! If each of us has the knowledge of the whole, and is capable of becoming identical to the whole, does that mean we already know all there is to know? As God does? Can that be right? Are we potentially God? Surely . . ."

"What do you think?"

We talked about scriptures that have had such a terrible time trying to explain to us who we are. They have to end up telling us who God is and how God works, but they're really talking about us. "Without beginning, without end . . . ?"

"God is everywhere—He is in all things—Master of all the universes—I can't think of a passage anywhere that any of this would contradict."

We were embracing each other. It felt so good to be so close to him.

"What a day you must have had! What a story!"

"Hey, if I get another invitation, would you like to go? I'll call and you can hop the next plane out."

The thought of it made him pause. "You'd want me to go there with you? Me?"

"Of course you, Papa. Who else in the world would I want more to share it with than you? Isn't that what we've been doing all day? Didn't we go there together today?"

"It's too good to be true," he said, shaking his head. "It's just too good to be true."

We talked of lots of things that afternoon, and we both knew that no matter what we said, whatever we talked about would eventually lead to the subject of death. His death. We also knew we could talk about it openly and without fear.

"What do you think happens when one 'dies,' so to speak?" he asked thoughtfully. "That is, we know we have life forever. But I wonder what takes place at that moment. How does it happen? Where do we go, and how do we get there?"

We talked about the book *Life After Death*, followed by Raymond Moody's book, *Life After Life*. We agreed the latter was the more accurate term, that both of its meanings were appropriate to the subject.

Both books included scores of interviews with persons who had been through the near-death experience, once sloughed off by laymen and professionals alike as mere "hallucinations of the unbalanced." That is, until more and more perfectly normal and sane people began coming forward to tell their stories. And it turns out that most accounts have at the least had an uncanny similarity, many are identical, and all are far too similar in detail to ignore.

I finally said to Papa, "The way I've come to understand it, all universes and everything in them move in cycles, and we're no exception. Instead of death, there's only change. So we just keep getting recycled over and over and over again till we've experienced every single facet of human life and learned how to meet it all with love. Then we get to go live and work as part of the big Master Thought and be in all space at all times everywhere—free from all these confining laws of Time and Space." I had to laugh. "But in the meantime, life is a lot like being in the third grade—we just keep doing it over and over again till we get it right.

"Papa, you know beyond a shadow of doubt there's no such thing as death. Because that's just foolishness, and not the way creation is set up. Now you can laugh at death as being anything more than a myth."

"Well, that's what the Master said. And I always believed—although I guess I never understood it like I do now." He thought for a moment and added, "I can't share this with anyone, you know. They'd call me crazy!"

"It's all yours. You don't need to tell anyone."

The sun was getting low in the sky, and I walked to the window to pull the blind.

"Never mind," he said. "Let the sun come in. I think I appreciate it more right now than ever before."

We sat silently for ever so long a time before he spoke again. Gazing out the window, he said, "I know dying must be merely going out of one place into another, not even losing consciousness—just lifting out of the body and leaving it behind."

"That's all it is, Papa. It's just too absurd to think that the consciousness that we are can ever die; we always have been and always will be living, conscious entities. Physical things die; consciousness survives forever—throughout infinite time—cycle after cycle after cycle."

"I never did believe that it was a final thing, you know," he confessed, "so I've never been afraid of it in that sense. When the time comes, though, I know I'll probably fight like a son-of-a-gun to stay, because it will be so hard to leave Grace Lee and you girls. You're the most important things in my life."

"Death is always worse for those left behind."

"Yes, we've seen a lot of that, haven't we?"

"Death is far from being the worst thing that can happen to a person.

It's actually fear of the unknown that panics people so, when it seems to me, God has saved the best for last. You and I, we pretty well understand, and we don't have to fight it like so many others we know."

"It's so unnecessary, isn't it?"

"Absolutely. And you know that when the time comes, there are those who'll cling to you and hold on desperately, as if they could make you stay longer by their tears. They don't realize that they're making it that much more difficult for the person making the transition. But I give you this promise right now, Papa, that I *will* let you go. There's no need to tell you how much I wish you'd stay, because you know that no one loves you more than I. But when you're ready, I'll not make it any harder for you than it already is. When it's time, it's time. You go, and bon voyage."

He nodded. "I understand what you're telling me, and I appreciate it. And will you do all you can to make Grace Lee and Joniece understand that I don't want them to grieve and linger over my passing—that they must go on with their lives?"

"It'll be hard to make them hear, but I'll do my best. At least it won't be like when some people go, the ones left behind being filled with such anguish and guilt that they didn't love the person enough, or didn't give them all they feel they should have given them. We couldn't feel that way about you, Papa. We've been too close. Regardless of who goes first, that feeling just won't be there."

"Thank you, honey. It's true that I don't feel the least bit cheated by life. It's been so good to me in every way!"

"You've never cheated life, Pop. So how could it cheat you?"

He closed his eyes and smiled. "I want to tell you something I'm feeling right now, Donna. The things we've talked about today we've never said before. But somehow it's all sort of strangely familiar to me. I don't know how to explain it."

"You don't have to. Don't you see—it's because the real 'you' is actually a cell of God, and God knows everything there is to know. So you see, there's no such thing as 'learn.' We can only 'remember.'"

"I feel in my heart that's true. It sounds so right. It's sort of ringing some old familiar bells somewhere inside my head, you know?"

"Yeah. You bet I do. I spent one day remembering who I am. But you've spent your whole life remembering who you are by looking at problems as just opportunities to love and serve—because something way back in your memory says that's how to get it all done right so you can go home."

"I wasn't conscious of that, but I see what you mean. Donna, I feel you have a good understanding of some very high truths. Thank you for sharing them with me today."

"Thanks for letting me, Papa."

"You girls have been such a blessing to me, you and Joniece. I couldn't have chosen more beautiful and loving children. Joniece is such a good person, and a truly fine artist. I'm so proud of her! I love you both so much."

Closing his eyes, he lay back on his pillow. "Keep remembering, Donna, and never become lazy. You have such a fine mind. Both of you girls are so . . ."

I sat quietly and watched my father's once handsome face as his breathing became even and rhythmic. I was as much at peace as he was. I kissed his big gentle hand.

The room by now was in near darkness, so I tiptoed to the window to pull the blind for the night. But I stopped when I saw the crescent sliver of a moon in the west where the sun had been. It would give him such pleasure to discover it, should he awaken during the night.

I quietly opened the door to remove his humorous DO NOT DISTURB sign. No, it would stay where he put it. He didn't need a pill to keep him awake today, nor did he need one to put him to sleep tonight.

"Good night, Papa," I whispered. "I love you . . ."

CHAPTER 17

*U*pon my return to Los Angeles, I accepted a job as executive secretary in a Beverly Hills firm. And it was at work one November afternoon when there came a quiet knock at my door. The receptionist timidly apologized for the interruption, but my mother was on the line.

"Hello—Mom?"

There was a painful silence at the other end.

"Honey," she choked, "when can you come home? Daddy's not going to be with us much longer."

After a moment I said, "I'll check with the airlines, Mom. I'll call you when I get home and let you know when to meet me. Mom?" What words could I say to her now? My mind was scrambling for anything.

"Hold on, Mom. We knew this was coming, didn't we?" I asked softly. "Well, so here we are. It's okay, Mom. Everything's happening just the way it's supposed to. Not the way we want it to, but the way it's really supposed to. I guess it's time, Mom."

I knew my words had no effect on her, but at that moment it was necessary that I verbally confirm my own faith.

I finished Mr. Weil's dictation and stayed an extra hour to complete his letters and documents and then called the airlines. There were several flights, but anything that late would necessitate changing planes, enduring layovers, and arriving in the middle of the night. So I made a reservation for early the next morning and drove back to my apartment to pack.

There was no guessing how long I would be away, so I over-packed, set the alarm, and tried to fall asleep.

At three A.M. I was still wide awake. I got out of bed, slipped into my sneakers and threw my sailing jacket around my shoulders.

One of the pleasures of living in Marina del Rey was that immediately behind my apartment building began an almost mile-long jetty banking the south side of the main channel which took the boats out to sea. At the very end was a lighthouse, and it was my habit to walk it almost daily. There I had enjoyed many sunrises, sunsets, and bike rides. But tonight was not the same as ever before.

I strolled aimlessly toward the lighthouse as the breeze from the ocean played with my hair. My mind had been so cluttered when I lay in bed only a few minutes ago. I wondered why I could now think of nothing to think about.

I reached the end of the jetty. Colossal boulders were piled into an enormous mound upon which sat the lighthouse. I climbed up onto the huge concrete base and sat with my feet dangling, looking out into a black sea. The water before me was calm. But I could hear the waves crashing on the far side of the breakwater.

"It's the same ocean that only a few yards away is furiously dashing itself against the rocks," I thought. "The breakwater is a buffer, so the channel can enjoy peaceful waters."

From the time I had left work, an uncomfortable ache had worked its way into my chest. It was so subtle and gradual that I had not become aware of the weight of it until now.

I closed my eyes and breathed in deeply the sea air. The weight grew, and I knew I had begun what months before I had promised my father I would not do—I was holding on to him. I resolved to release my father then and there.

More deep breathing. Relax and let go. Must find that place inside with all the space. Answers are always there when I can relax and expand. God is in that space. More of God. Expand. Pull more space into the lungs and into the mind. More deep breathing. Let go. Let go. Ah . . . then time was not.

Quite suddenly I became aware of a presence standing beside me to my right. But my eyes remained closed and my body relaxed. I waited.

"Let not your heart be troubled, child. Go forward and do what you must do. Your understanding is greater than you think. Everything is proceeding according to plan."

I slowly opened my eyes and turned my head in the direction of the voice. But my finite eyes saw precisely what they knew they would see—nothing at all.

The voice had spoken so lovingly, with such reassurance and authority. And now the words echoed softly inside my head. The weight had been lifted from me. My father was at last free. And so was I.

I wept hard for my mother.

*J*oniece met my plane. She told me what little there was to know on the way to the hospital. It was only a matter of time. "But he's not in pain, Donna. Isn't that wonderful?" she tried consoling us both. "He's heavily sedated, so he's not in pain."

"Is he awake?"

"Now and then—off and on." She added, "Mom's not doing too well."

"So how are you holding up, love?"

"Oh, I'm fine. The hardest thing I've had to do is keep up the work at the plant, do two TV shows this week, and run back and forth to the hospital every few hours. You know, I guess everyone at the plant senses that this is it. And between 'How's your father' and 'I'm so sorry,' they're asking me for decisions I've never had to make before.

"Here I am, about to leap into a position I've wanted since I was five years old. Everyone knows I'm going to step in when he's gone. And I know I can do it, but . . ." She was biting her lip hard.

"My god, Donna, I just didn't know it would be this way. How in the devil am I supposed to take over this big company, while Daddy's lying there . . ."

I finished it for her. "Dying." I turned away and looked out the window at nothing in particular. Guilt began to consume me. Who in the world did I think I was anyway? I had selfishly left home when I was young and gone out to "see the world!" Wow. Had I copped out! With any foresight at all, I would have known that my family would need me to be here one day to help with the business. Now the time had come, and I was totally unprepared and useless to them. Joniece was left to bear the entire burden alone. I wanted to scream, but I continued to stare out the window until we arrived at the hospital.

Mom was in the hallway. We clung to each other for a long time.

She then led me into Papa's room and said, "John . . . sweetheart . . . Donna's here."

His head jerked in my direction. Although he couldn't open his eyes, his hand reached out to me. I took his big hand in both of mine, and he squeezed with all of what was left of his might.

"Oh, honey . . . I'm so glad you're here." His voice was a whimper. "I've been awful sick. I sure want to go home, baby. Would you take me home?"

I explained as one would to a child that here they could give him better care and keep a close watch on him, that for now it was best for him to remain where he was. I hoped he didn't hear the hurt in my voice. But he had already slipped back into sleep from the sedative.

It was Tuesday. How long would he be this way? How much longer before he would leave us?

"He can't remain too much longer," Dr. Martin advised us. "His blood pressure is down to almost nothing."

Every four hours he was roused long enough to take the pills that would put him back to sleep. He labored to swallow them. But he never failed to thank the nurses.

There was a constant presence of hospital staff in his room and outside his door. From all departments, at all hours, they used their breaks to come and check on "their Mr. Frank." Many of the nurses and aides were very religious and came to pray at the foot of his bed.

Through all the pain and discomforts he suffered, not once did he say a cross word or fail to thank the ladies who did any small thing to make him more comfortable. Even when the medicine was bitter, he took it without complaint, hoping it would make him well so he could go home.

I replaced the night nurse at seven o'clock on Sunday morning. As I walked into his room, three nurses were trying to sit him up to take his medication, but he could not respond.

"Don't. Please. No more pills from now on. Just let him be," I said. They nodded as if they were relieved to hear the words, and they left the room. It didn't take a doctor to see he was going into a coma. I made the decision not to call Mom or Joniece. Later. Let them rest.

I sat down beside his bed and watched him for a long time and listened to him breathe. I have always known that even when a person is unconscious, even when the body cannot respond, the essence, or soul, is alert and hears and understands everything. I began to talk to him.

"Hey, Papa . . . I know you can hear me, Papa . . . so listen. I want you to know I'm keeping my promise to you. I mean, it's okay with me any time you want to check out. I'm not holding on."

I told him the story of that night at the lighthouse and the voice that had spoken to me. When I finished, he took a deep breath and sighed. I knew he had heard me.

"Soon Mom and Johnnie will be here. And I'm going to have to break it to them that you're about ready, you know? Mom's going to be okay, I know she'll be. It's just a great big shock trying to think about you not being around. I guess she's awfully scared.

"Johnnie is, too, only in a different way. But you know how well you've taught her, and she's going to be just great when she gets the hang of it. We've all got a lot of shock to get over, Pop. You're going to leave such a giant space behind you . . .

"Now, you know I'm okay—because we said everything we ever needed to say to each other last summer, remember? You're going to be so happy to get rid of this sick old body that's caused you such pain and held you down for such a long time.

"You and I know what's happening. We know that death is simply another birth into a new life—just like when an acorn stops being an acorn and starts being a tree. I know you're not afraid to let go of this part of your life and go on to the next stage. After all, Papa, you made such an adventure out of this one—with no fear of anyone or anything—I know when you get to the other side you'll find some fun to stir up there, too."

I began to reflect. "Hey, Papa, remember what you told me once a long time ago? One day a few years ago, you said, 'Honey, I've done everything in life I ever set out to do.' You leaned back in your easy chair with the most satisfied smile. Then you laughed out loud and said, 'Everything from now on is just cream on the top!'

"I was so proud of you. Boy, was I proud! I thought, how many others in the world can say that. But then, how many people ever learn how to let go of all those things that keep them from living fully?

"Remember all the times you were told that if you supported this cause or that project you'd not only lose your business, you'd be run out of town on a rail? I watched you laugh and go at it with twice the fury, just to prove they were wrong. And you sure did it, Papa. People just stood aside and said, 'Make way for da bossman!'" I laughed out loud. And I knew he was laughing with me.

"You fought hard for whatever it was you believed in, whether it turned out in the end to be right or not. God Himself, you said, never expects more of us than that. It's not what we do, but the way we do it and our reasons for doing it that count."

There was something I hadn't yet told him. I had recently walked away from show business and burned all those proverbial bridges behind me. I knew at last what it was like to be gently and positively guided in a new direction. This would be my last opportunity to share it with him.

"Papa, I've been wanting to tell you this. I told you I wanted to be a physician. But I just can't come up with the money or the time it would take to get there. But now I know I'm supposed to be writing. Yeah—books! I'm going to be writing about those universal laws we talked about that day when I visited you at St. Francis. But I've remembered so often what you said—'You're the only book some people read.' So I won't talk about anything I'm not an example of, just like you. I promise.

"I'm discovering all the time a lot more of the laws like we talked about that day. And it's true what you said—there's no limit, not even the sky.

"I can say these things to you, because you know I'm coming from the same place you are. And, like you, I need to pass it on to anyone who'll listen. I think I can say it in such a way that those who really want to understand can grasp it if they try.

"So many people are turned off by the word 'God,' because they're still working from an image they had when they were a child, and their understanding didn't grow up when they did. But I believe I can change those images and show them that God, in reality, is an intelligent energy, a frequency, something that fills all space everywhere, not some bearded figure up there writing our life scenarios for us.

"I think just maybe I can change the way people understand the laws. They really do work, you know, when they're fully and faithfully practiced. People should know that the universe is here to work for them, not against them. We have access to all the keys. We just need to understand the meaning of the words, instead of writing them off as so much religious nonsense.

"The laws never change. They work just the same today as they did billions of years ago. Only man's laws change. When we know that power is available to us right here and now, then everything we need and want is ours—that 'abundance' you always preached to us about."

My father was hearing every word. He gave another heavy sigh, and I thought he smiled.

I sat back and laughed at myself for having felt the need to say all of that. My father was the book that many thousands of people had already read and learned so much about successful living from. His life had been proof of those very universal laws that I would one day write about.

Then I knew. Of course. My first book would be the story of him.

Why had it taken so long for the light to come on? I was forty-one years old, and the best teacher I could have had was right under my nose. I had to go out and fight my way through the entire world, from shore to bleeding shore, lesson after excruciating lesson, to finally come up with what he had tried all along to show me. Just recognize that everyone is God in disguise, and then love and serve that person accordingly. Is that what he meant by "serving God by serving people?" Could it be that simple?

Deeply embarrassed and humiliated at seeing clearly my own life's melodrama, I sat with my face in my hands. I felt heavy and chilled.

"Now I can see it, Papa. Now I can go on with my work—remembering who I am—by remembering that every pair of eyes I look into are God's eyes. I suppose that's about all I have to do from now on, isn't it?"

I breathed deeply and tried hard to let go of my remorse. It wasn't necessary to feel that in my father's presence. He understood, and he loved me anyway.

Soon a gentle warmth began to settle around and through me. I looked at my father's face and felt a profound and complete love union with him, one that we had never approached in all those years that he was physically well and conscious.

I knelt down beside his bed. I put my head on his familiar arm and closed my eyes.

"I hear you, Papa. At long last, I do hear you. Forgive me for being so blind all this time." I was sure the room had begun to glow. "Thanks for not giving up on me. I love you, Papa."

I relaxed and bathed for a long while in the warmth of his presence. I thought I felt a hand on my shoulder.

CHAPTER 18

My mother and sister arrived mid-morning after a good rest. I stopped them before they entered the room and asked them to first sit down outside.

I fumbled for words, and then finally came out quite simply with, "Dad went into a coma when I arrived this morning, and he's not coming out. There was nothing you could do, so I decided to let you sleep."

For a few moments we all cried quietly. Then resignedly we rose and entered his room.

We sat for a while, feeling helpless, watching his labored, regular breathing. My sister spoke first. "You can leave, Daddy. It's okay. We all understand. Don't stay and suffer, Daddy. Please don't suffer. We'd do anything in the world if we could have you back, but we don't want you to be sick and hurting." She held his hand and kissed him on the forehead. He heard but could not respond.

Then a light came into my sister's face. "He's waiting for someone. He won't leave until somebody gets here!"

She looked at Mother and me. I nodded, feeling she had hit upon what was keeping him earthbound. Indeed he was waiting for someone. But who? We could only be patient and wait.

The stream of well-wishers had grown daily. The halls were filled to overflowing with people who loved him, coming to say good-bye and offering whatever comforting words or services they could. Waves of people arrived and replaced the waves of people that were leaving.

I spent much of the day searching for words that my mother could possibly hear.

"Do you realize how fortunate you are, Mother? You've had forty-five years with the only man you ever loved. And how he has loved you! A lot of good women have envied you that. Forty-five years of happiness and creativity most people never even get a taste of. That's a lot to take pride in and say thank you for."

I held her hand till I thought she could hear more.

"When we cry, we always cry for ourselves, because we're afraid of what it will be like living without Papa. But loving him also means we must look at his life and see exactly what he was trying to tell us by his example.

"See, we're sitting around out here all bottled up with fear, and he's lying in there calm and cool as can be. He knows perfectly well what he's doing, and he's not in the least afraid to do it. He knows there's more to fear in life than in death. Papa won hands down over fear in life, so you know he's not afraid of death. He knew that one really well, didn't he?"

Mother began to relax a little.

"Dad and I once talked about this thing people call death. And we agreed we simply couldn't buy it, that it just isn't real. After all, that was one of the main things the Master tried to teach us. And most of us are so blind we can't see it.

"When things are going well, we say we believe. Then when it comes down to the wire, we forget to use our faith when we're supposed to. This is the real test, right now. Here we are. And now is the time to believe.

"Mom, a very important part of loving is being able to let go when it's time. Papa doesn't want you to sit around and grieve. He wants you to go on living like the happy person you really and truly are, with or without him. If you can do that, he'll be so pleased and so proud of you."

She stared straight ahead, and I felt a bit of strength come back into her. She took a breath and relaxed a little more. She shook her head slowly, and a faint smile appeared.

"You certainly are your father's daughter. You and John together have enough faith for all of us. I've never seen anything like it."

I looked toward Papa's room and saw my sister, whom I had been watching from the corner of my eye. "And speaking of Father's daughter," I said, "just look at her. She really has it together on that end, hasn't she?"

Johnnie was doing exactly as Papa would have done in the same situation. She was greeting people, accepting their loving concern in a most gracious way, and efficiently handling the traffic without being in the least rude.

"She's so much like him, isn't she?" Mother mused. "You two girls are such opposites. And yet you're both so like your father. Isn't it odd?"

We were interrupted by the entrance of Rev. Robert Fraley. Papa loved and admired this man, and they had shared a deep friendship. Joniece came forward and greeted him warmly.

"Bob, you may be the one he wants to see. Come with me."

Looking a bit puzzled, Bob was led into Dad's room. Joniece politely asked that the room be cleared, and all obeyed.

Joniece then took Papa's hand and said, "Daddy, Bob Fraley is here to see you . . ." Minutes went by as they listened to him breathe.

Bob then closed his eyes and offered a prayer that conveyed his love and asked that God's will, above all, be done, and they walked back out into the hallway.

"He's waiting for someone, Bob, and I thought it might be you. I'm sorry if I startled you."

The day brought several other similar incidents. But Papa stubbornly held on.

At ten o'clock that night, I persuaded Mother to let me take her home to rest, as this could go on indefinitely. Although my sister showed utter fatigue, she insisted she wanted to remain for a few minutes more. The corridor had been cleared, and most of the lights had been turned off. We reluctantly left her in a lonely corner of the hall and drove home.

Joniece went over in her mind every person that had been there that day and pondered who had been missing. "It must be someone he won't leave without saying goodbye to. I wonder . . ."

A tall figure in a hunting jacket and boots tiptoed down the corridor. He spotted Joniece sitting in the dark corner and came toward her.

"I came as soon as I heard, Joniece. I was up at the lake when . . ."

"Oh, Dave! I'm so glad you're here! You're the one he wants to see. Come with me."

Dave Cox, Director of the Tulsa Youth for Christ, turned ashen when he heard her words, and he hesitantly followed her into the room.

Together they took the once quick hand that now lay limp on his chest, and Joniece announced with confidence, "Daddy, your boy Dave is here . . ."

A look of peace came over our father's face like a benediction. With one long sigh, they watched him gently let go. My sister looked at the clock and made a mental note of the time.

The two stood motionless and observed the empty, lifeless shell they held. After a long silence, Joniece began knowingly to explain.

"Dave, the two most important legacies that Daddy has are Frankoma and Youth for Christ. He had to pass the light on to each of us—Frankoma to me, and YFC to you. He just wouldn't leave without knowing we understood that."

Dave and Joniece walked out into the half-light of the corridor, and Dave awkwardly began to speak.

"When we made that last turn coming into town a few minutes ago, I told my wife I'd take her home before I went to the hospital to see John, because I didn't know how long I'd be. She argued that I shouldn't take the time, that I might get there too late. But I told her it was all right, because he won't go till I get there.

"She looked at me real funny and asked me how I knew that. And I said, 'He told me back at that last turn coming into town.'"

The two stared ahead, and Joniece gently nodded her head and whispered, "Yes. Of course."

"Now, Johnnie, I can't really explain how I heard it, but it was like way deep inside my head. I heard him tell me that just as plain as can be. Do you think I'm crazy?"

"Dave, after what just happened in there, do you think I'm going to question anything like that ever again?"

They said good night, and Joniece walked slowly down the hall to call us the news. It was November 10, 1973, and Papa had crossed over at precisely 10:20 P.M. It was days before we realized it was on November 10, 1938, that Frankoma had burned, and that the phone call had come at exactly 10:20 P.M. He had departed thirty-five years later, to the minute.

CHAPTER   1 9

*I*n the following two and a half days before the funeral, we estimate that more than eight hundred people came to our home to express their sympathy. Various clubs, organizations, and churches showed their love and concern by bringing food enough to feed a multitude and, like the story of the loaves and fishes, it seemed there was more left over than what we had started with.

We could have used a secretary to receive phone calls alone, as it seemed the phone never stopped ringing. At night we took the receiver off the hook so Mother could sleep. We were all quite exhausted.

My husband arrived from Los Angeles by plane on Monday afternoon. As he entered the house, a group of friends were leaving for the funeral home, and he asked if he might ride with them.

When our friends had paid their respects to Papa, Gus told them to leave without him.

The parlor was empty but for Gus and Papa. They had been good friends, and in many respects Gus had regarded Papa as his teacher. He smiled when he saw that we had chosen to dress Papa in his favorite jacket—"my foxy red one," he called it. It was maroon with a black paisley design. And in the lapel was his diamond Rotary pin of which he was so proud.

Gus sat quietly as if he were searching for something to say. But it was Papa who had something to tell Gus. In a few moments, Gus rose and stepped out into the chill November twilight and began walking briskly toward home.

There wasn't a breath of wind, but one or two low branches of each tree swayed gently as he passed it. It made him smile, and it also made him shiver a little.

It was about a two-mile walk. Gus came down the long hill that approached the house, admiring the terracing, each rock of which Papa had put into place with his own hands. Everything he saw had known Papa's touch. He hesitated before walking up the driveway. Instead, he turned to follow the outside of the semi-circular house and walked down the hill, down the stepped terracing to the orchard.

He remembered the day they met. Gus had hitchhiked more than half the length of the country to ask me to marry him. Dad tossed his head and laughed appreciatively when Gus told him, "You have a really happy house, Mr. Frank. It's even shaped like a grin!"

Gus continued to stroll about until he had covered all the ground that Papa had loved so well. It looked neglected and in need of the master's care. The trees and shrubs seemed to know well their loss.

I met my husband at the door. He put his arm around me, and his eyes filled with tears. But he was smiling.

"John wanted so very much to make that walk home. I let him use me. He was so happy! We walked all over the grounds together and . . ." He turned and walked into the other room and closed the door to be alone.

*T*uesday came. The phone sounded bright and early, and I answered to hear a voice ask if he could speak to a member of the family. I introduced myself, and the gentleman began to tell me of a night years ago when he and his family were driving along Highway 75 about ten miles from the nearest town when their car broke down. It was very late, and no one would stop to help or give him a ride. Though fearful of leaving his wife and children in the car, he had no choice but to begin the long walk back to town.

Soon a big green Chrysler convertible whizzed past him. It screeched to a stop, backed up, and the driver said, "What's the trouble, my friend?"

The man drove him the ten miles back into town, but every garage they found was closed. Not in the least discouraged, the man drove around until he found a phone booth. He awakened an old friend who lived there and inquired as to who was the best mechanic in town, and where he lived.

The two men roused the mechanic out of a sound asleep and insisted that he promptly drive out to the car on the highway and fix it. The man's stubborn refusal was softened when he was handed a large denomination bill to more than pay him for his trouble.

"Ma'am, your father was a saint. I didn't even know who he was till he was leaving. It wasn't till then that we shook hands and introduced ourselves, and I learned it was Mr. Frank who'd been my Good Samaritan. I asked him why he'd bothered to stop for a man like me. He told me he just had a feeling about me and had to stop. And I said I was praying when I saw him coming that he would.

"Ma'am, I'm the pastor of a small church here in Tulsa. Your father came and talked to our church not long after that, and he's been so special to me and my congregation ever since then. Do you suppose it would be all right if I came to the funeral this afternoon?"

"Of course you may, sir," I assured him. "Why do you even ask?"

"Well, I'm black, you know. And I thought maybe . . . "

I laughed. Sir, if you were a friend of Dad's, we would be honored. The funeral is at two o'clock at the Methodist Church on Taft, and we'll expect you. God bless you, sir."

"Thank you very much, ma'am. I'll be there on behalf of my congregation. They loved him a lot, too."

Dark, heavy clouds moved at low altitude, churned by a cold, driving wind. "It should be calm and sunny for Papa's grand exit," I thought. "Why must it be so dark?"

The parking lot was overflowing, and there were no spaces to be found for half a mile on either side of the First United Methodist Church. The hallways were filled, and there was no standing room left in the church. I wondered if there were many persons standing outside the door.

A large platform supported the podium and the altar, behind which rose a giant ceramic cross that Papa had specially created and placed with his own hands when the church was built. Tall, narrow panels of brilliant stained glass windows rose on either side of the podium and surrounded the large sanctuary.

In the first window to the right of the platform was a long, slender, four-pointed star. The service had barely begun when quite suddenly the sun burst through the clouds and exploded its light into the sanctuary directly through the center of that golden star!

An audible gasp rose in unison from the crowd, and all eyes were fixed on the star for several breathless moments until a cloud slowly covered its brilliance and it faded. It was the sun's only appearance that day.

Ceramic cross. Sapulpa, Oklahoma. Created by John Frank in 1967 for the First United Methodist Church.

As the service resumed, I glanced round. There were teenage girls in miniskirts, young boys in football jackets, little old women in flowered hats, men in suits that had seen better days, Salvation Army uniforms, ladies in expensive furs, diamond-fingered bankers, farmers, and clerical collars.

"What a melting pot!" I whispered to my husband out of the corner of my mouth. And at that moment, as I had experienced a thousand times before, there was a playful shove, strong enough to push me into Gus' arm. He was as shocked as I was, and his look reprimanded me for my irreverent behavior. I could only give him an apologetic look and shrug my shoulders. My father was free, and his tremendous energies had been released.

"It's him, honey—he's just playing around," I said, trying to explain. He gave me a frown, and we resumed staring ahead.

"Okay, Pop, now settle down," I thought. "You don't have to be serious, but we do." I had to smile, though. He was enjoying the parade, and I could feel the familiar playfulness of him all around me.

Days later we were to learn that my sister's close friend, of whom my father was especially fond, had the same experience while standing at the back of the church. She recognized the familiar friendly nudge, and it so frightened her, she had to lean against the wall to keep from fainting.

A long time friend of Papa's delivered the eulogy, and the choir sang his favorite hymn, "Have Thine own way, Lord, have Thine own way; Thou art the potter, I am the clay . . ." After the benediction, the casket was moved to the exit so that people could say their goodbyes as they left the sanctuary. We, the family, were to wait for everyone else to leave before we made our exit.

It seemed hours before the crowd began to thin. No one simply walked by to look. Almost without exception, each stopped to touch him and say a word to him.

A young girl took his hands and said, "Thank you, Mr. Frank, for all you did."

A leather-faced farmer stopped to say, "My wife and I couldn't have made it that year without your help. God bless you, Mr. Frank," and turned away to cover his tearful face with a faded bandanna handkerchief.

An elderly black woman, surely in her nineties, cried unashamedly and fumbled with her crutch as she reached out to stroke his forehead and smooth his hair. "I'm comin' soon, John. I'm right behind ya, John. God bless ya, John . . ."

I was curious to know the stories behind all these goodbyes. There were scores to wonder about as we waited.

I watched a prominent, superbly dressed woman lay her head on his chest and sob without restraint. She had to be led away.

A pretty white-haired lady in a Salvation Army uniform put her hand on his and said simply, "We'll miss you, John. There'll never be another like you."

I saw a portly black gentleman whom I recognized to be the minister of a nearby church to which Papa had given a hundred or more plates for church socials. He looked long and lovingly at Papa and said aloud, "God has surely received you with love, Mr. Frank. I know you're with God."

There was a young man in an army uniform whom Papa had taught in Sunday School as a boy. His hands grasped the side of the casket and he leaned over closely, as if to make sure he would be heard. "I remember everything you said, Mr. Frank. Thanks for all you taught us kids."

No one was in a hurry to say goodbye to the Man of the Day, and all took their time. I found myself crying too, but for them, because they thought he was gone. I knew very well my father was right there watching and listening, pouring out upon each of them the same abundant love, now as before. I wondered if anyone else felt his eminent presence. Perhaps they did. Maybe that was what allowed each of them to speak to him so freely.

*T*he limousine pulled up in front of the new mausoleum south of town. Johnnie and I helped our mother into the building and took our places down front.

A delegation from the Creek Nation had called to ask permission to say a prayer before he was interred. We had of course welcomed them to say a farewell in their own tongue to their honorary brother White Eagle.

A stout gentleman appeared and boldly stood before us. His Indian beads and jewelry blended magnificently well with a tailored business suit. He was broadly built, his face was square and brave, and his skin a dark bronze. It occurred to me that he could have posed for the Indian head nickel.

Reverend Jonas Partridge raised his right hand with impressive authority and closed his eyes. His voice rang out in rich, deep tones and sent a shiver through the crowd. Although few knew the Creek words he spoke, not a soul doubted what he was asking of the Great Spirit, as we saw tears flow down Jonas' face. Each person felt the dynamic power and sentiment of the staccato Creek syllables.

A small bouquet was placed beneath our father's pillow. There were kernels of Indian corn for him to eat on the way; there was Indian tobacco, whose smoke would carry his prayers to the Great Spirit Father; there was a vial of fresh spring water; and a feather to help wing his way to the Happy Hunting Grounds.

"It's perfect," I thought. "The perfect ending to this chapter in a long, eternal life."

And the lid was closed for the last time.

*F*or several more days I stayed with my mother, as she was not yet ready to face being all alone in the house she and Papa had dreamed of and built together. I answered some of the many phone calls that came day and night as the news about Papa spread across the country.

Joniece was forced to carry the sorrow of her father's passing while being thrown headlong into her new role at Frankoma. It was not an easy adjustment for her.

Letters and cards arrived in such volume that the post office delivered them in large mail sacks.

There were letters and telegrams from President and Mrs. Nixon, Speaker of the House Carl Albert, governors, senators, and representatives. There were letters from people we knew, and many from those whose lives only Papa had touched. Dozens carried stories he had never told anyone. And in this way, parts of our father's life were slowly unfolded to us, and we began to know much more about him than we had ever known before.

*O*ne letter told of a plane ride some years back. A college student sat next to my father, and they began a friendly conversation.

The young man was a member of Youth for Christ in a New England state. He was delighted to learn that he was sitting with John Frank, whose name he knew and admired not only through YFC, but through his work as an artist as well.

During their flight together the young man revealed that he had wanted very much to become a professional artist, but the small junior college where he was enrolled did not have an art department, and finances would not permit him to go elsewhere to study.

My father wrote the boy's name and address in his little book and remarked that they just might meet again one day.

Almost a year later Papa flew to that state to speak at a church conference. After the meeting, he rented a car and drove some distance to the small college of which the boy on the plane had spoken. He inquired as to why there was no art department and was told that the college was too small to support a department in which there was insufficient interest.

John Frank questioned that answer and persuaded one of the teachers to conduct a poll to determine just exactly what interest actually did exist among the students. To the surprise of the entire faculty, there was an overwhelming response in the positive, and my father pledged a sizeable sum of money to help create the new department.

The art classes at that college were soon full to overflowing. And who later became the director of the art department? You guessed it—the young man on the plane.

*J*ohn Frank had once been driving through a small town in Texas when he stopped at a service station for gas. A little boy approached him and asked if he would buy a raffle ticket for a quarter to raise money for a new Little League baseball team.

"What do I get if I win?" my father asked the child.

"Five dollars I think, mister."

"Five dollars? That's not enough to make me want to buy a ticket.

You should have a better prize than that, don't you think?"

The little boy giggled shyly and asked, "Don't you wanna buy a ticket?"

Papa thought about it a minute and said, "How many you got there?"

"I got this whole book. I ain't sold none yet."

"Okay, I'll take the whole book. But now tell me who's in charge of your Little League."

The barefoot boy took the money with wide eyes and gave him the name of a pharmacist down the street. Papa drove to the drugstore and introduced himself to the man behind the counter.

"I hear you're about to get a Little League team started here. That right?"

"Yeah, the kids need something to keep 'em out of trouble during the summer. I love kids, and I just took it upon myself to help get a team going."

"May I use your phone? It's a long distance call, but I'll make it collect. Oh, and I'd like one of your cards please. May I?"

"Sure, mister. Help yourself."

Papa called the plant and asked his secretary to send a set of Wagon Wheel dishes to this address and "charge it to promotion!" It had to be taken to the express office right away in order to get it onto the next truck. It was imperative that it arrive at this address as soon as possible.

Three days later it was no problem for the Little Leaguers to sell their tickets. Everyone in the small Texas town was eager to win a set of Frankoma Wagon Wheel dishes!

One of the nurses caring for my father had stopped me in the hallway the day before he died. She took me aside and told me that she had met my father six years ago when he came to speak at the small church she attended.

"I know he was sent to me from God. I told Mr. Frank I wanted more than anything to be a nurse, but that I had to drop out of school because my daddy died, and I had to work to support my mother. He told me to go back to school right then, not to wait.

"He made me promise not to tell anyone where the money came

from, and then he paid off what we owed on Daddy's funeral. He also said I mustn't try to pay it back. And that's not all . . ." The young woman began to weep as if she were being relieved of a tremendous weight.

"Then there was a check every month for five months till I graduated. Now I'm making enough to live on and take care of my mother, too."

She dried her eyes and took my hand. "You understand, don't you? I'm only breaking my word to him now because he'll be gone soon, and I thought someone in his family ought to know."

I listened with interest to her story and thanked her for telling me. I remembered Lloyd C. Douglas' book, *Magnificent Obsession*, and how a doctor unlocked the "Source of Infinite Power" by helping people under the very same conditions, that his good deeds be kept secret and the money never repaid. "The investment of yourself in others. Once it becomes your way of life, you'll be bound. It will become an obsession—but it will be a magnificent obsession!"

Strange how clearly those words came back to me after so many years. Had Papa read the same book? Or had he come to discover this great secret on his own?

*L*ibby had been Frankoma's bookkeeper for many years. And for as long as she could remember, about once a week or so my father would go to her and ask for cash.

Sometimes he would tell her, "Libby, I'm taking a dozen gorgeous women to lunch today, so you'd better give me a hundred dollars to cover the tab."

She would laugh and take the cash from the safe. "Mr. Frank, it's your money. I don't care how you spend it."

More often than not, as soon as she gave it to him, he would hand it back to her. "When you go to the bank today, will you get me a money order for a hundred dollars? Oh, and don't say anything to anyone about this, huh?"

Or he would say, "Last month I charged a hundred and fifty dollars worth of fertilizer, and now those silly cows want their money, and I gotta have it to keep 'em quiet!"

Libby looked forward to the next zany story Papa would use as an excuse for the cash he wanted.

"Libby, I'm in trouble! The cops are after me, and I gotta disappear and lay low for a while! Can you slip me fifty?"

Each time Libby returned from the bank, Mr. Frank put a different name on the money order and slipped it into a hand-addressed envelope.

"Here, Libby, go put a stamp on this and shuffle it down to the bottom of the mail sack so nobody'll notice it. That's a good girl!"

Sometimes the check went to a person who had lost a member of the family and was unable to afford a decent burial. And sometimes it went to a farmer whose crop had failed and who had nowhere to turn until the next year's harvest.

Then there were those who were temporarily unemployed because of illness and were struggling to feed their families. Or there may have been elderly ladies who had lost husbands and needed help until their Social Security checks came through. Now and then a storm or a flood left a family homeless; or perhaps it was a fire that had wiped them out. But whatever their stores were, it didn't matter. To the extent that he was able, Papa would help them in whatever ways he could.

How did he learn about these people in need? What were his sources of information that told him when someone needed help? To this day we have no clue to the mystery. But we do know he made it a habit to seek them out and do what he could to help. And whenever possible, his giving was done in secret, with the condition that it never be repaid.

Now that he was gone, these stories could be told, and they were. And with every story that was revealed to me, the words I had forgotten came back: "Inasmuch as ye do it for the least of these, ye do it unto Me."

ollowing our father's passing, Joniece experienced
tremendous emotional struggles, as well as physical
stress, all part of learning to fine-tune the dynamics
of the business while also trying to keep up with
time-consuming design responsibilities. And in
her efforts to remain loyal to Papa's original concept of the Christmas
plate and perpetuate what he had begun years ago, Joniece had been
faced with numerous unique challenges.

Now, as she was settling in as both President and CEO of Frankoma
Pottery, she was making tough decisions on all levels of management.

It pleased me immensely that she had come through it all so well,
and I was proud of her courage and growth into her new role. She was
clearly a remarkable woman. I had known she was capable of doing it.
My faith in her abilities and talents had often surpassed her own.

John Frank had taught his apprentice well. And Joniece had
inherited a professional staff to be envied by all other manufacturers of
ceramics. Here was an unparalleled team of ceramic engineers and
experts that could, and did, accomplish every ambitious thing they set
out to do.

Joniece had knowledge of every department, and she kept all the
segments working together like a well-oiled machine. She was also
giving each of her supervisors more authority than they had ever
known, along with the freedom to expand and improve the efficiency of
their departments. They loved and respected her, and Frankoma
remained a happy and satisfied family that continued to grow under her
leadership.

In the summer of 1974, Joniece came to the Los Angeles Gift Show,
and we had one day together before she had to fly back to Oklahoma.

I had long since been divorced and now lived at the ocean in Venice,
and that afternoon we took a long, leisurely walk on the beach.

Later in the day, we lay quietly on the warm sand and watched the
sun sink below the calm Pacific horizon, accompanied by string of pink
and coral clouds that had flung themselves across the entire sky. As

dusk approached, we saw the first star appear in the western sky and watched until the heavens fairly danced with lights.

It was Joniece that finally broke the silence.

"Wouldn't you like to come back to Frankoma some day?" she asked hesitantly. "Mother will retire before long, and the retail department could be all yours. That's where the real money is, you know."

Uh-oh. The old guilt was suddenly back to haunt me, and I hated the bitter taste of it.

I forced a smile and avoided her look. "Can you—uh—possibly do without me?"

"Of course we can do without you, but—"

"I can't go back, Johnnie. Please understand. This is my home now, and I can't go back."

Her tears began to come. "Now I've got to say it and get it out," she cried. "I'm all set up back in Oklahoma—with a ready-made career and everything I ever wanted and dreamed of. And you have *nothing*! It's not fair, Donna! Please come home and take what's rightfully yours. You can have half the business and enough money to live any way you want."

Aha! Now the picture was coming into focus.

"You feel badly," I asked in genuine disbelief, "because you've got it all, and I have nothing?"

Johnnie nodded through her sobs. "Uh-huh . . ."

"Hey, stop it!" I exclaimed. "Let me tell you about what I've been suffering. I've been all choked up with guilt because you've had the whole burden dumped on you, and I've copped out by not being there to help you with the load. Do you hear what I'm saying? Do you see how both of us have been eaten up with guilt for nothing?"

My sister dried her eyes. "You mean you don't want to come back? You're really happy where you are?" She waved her hand about and made a face. "Here?"

"Johnnie, I'd go if I thought you desperately needed me. But quite honestly, I'm relieved to know everything's going so well. Because I love my cheap funky little pad by the sea, piled to the ceiling with books and ferns and sea shells and posters and furniture I built myself.

151

I'm deliriously happy here, because it's exactly where I want to be. This is me! I love it!"

Now she was laughing. "I've been so ashamed at having it all while you're being left out," she said. "I'm so glad it's okay with you that I'm running things back home."

"Okay?? Oh, Johnnie! I'm so grateful to you! If only I could tell you how thankful I am that you're there! Because if you weren't, I'd have to be doing it, and I'd be one heck of a wreck! I'd be a total misfit back there, trying to muddle my way through something I have absolutely no aptitude for! Don't you see?"

The water was now as black as the sky it was reflecting, and a gentle breeze from across the water reached us. We lay in silence and listened to the hypnotic sounds of Mother Ocean slowly breathing in and out, in and out.

Living so close to her, it had become such a familiar sound, constantly with me, awake or asleep, the ultimate reassurance that life goes on and on and on. The repetitive, rhythmic pulse of the Great Mother had permeated my senses and flowed through me for so long that, even when I was away from her, it was still going on inside me somewhere, so that her breath was my breath.

She had centered me so that I could expand. It was she who let me discover these new tools I could now work with—words—and without words she taught me how to use them. Thus I learned from her the Zen of writing. She instilled in me the confidence to be honest with myself, and allowed me to see that I was really *more* than who I thought I was. Mother Ocean had gifted me with that illusive, unnameable freedom that all my life I had longed for. How could I leave her?

"Wow, Donna," mused Joniece, "we've both suffered with this, haven't we? And all the time we've been exactly where we're supposed to be. Amazing. All this time. How could we have done this to ourselves?"

rankoma had grown to an impressive 79,000 square feet. There were five hydraulic presses on which were turned out as many as four thousand pieces of flatware daily, and as many items were also cast by hand. There were five huge tunnel kilns, operating around the clock, all year long. Approximately a million pieces of Frankoma Pottery were shipped annually to a national market and sold from its adjoining retail showroom.

Although it had evolved to a thoroughly modern operation in many respects, each piece was still trimmed, sponged, and glazed by human hands. In former years, when training his employees to do the hand work, John Frank retained only those who came to love, enjoy, and take pride in their work. He instinctively believed that the more persons that loved the piece they handled and processed, the more that feeling would be sensed by those who would later handle the finished product.

"Clay is alive!" he reminded them often. "And like all living things, it retains all the feelings put into it by those who take part in its creation and in bringing it to maturity."

By this time, there were salesmen in all the fifty states serving more than five thousand wholesale accounts, and as many as a quarter of a

Frankoma Pottery. Sapulpa, Oklahoma, c. 1982.
The plant is expanded to an impressive 79,000 square feet.

million visitors traveled each year to tour the home of Frankoma Pottery.

Now Frankoma's payroll totaled *daily* more than the sum of what Sapulpa's businessmen originally invested in John Frank's little pottery operation when he arrived in Sapulpa in 1938, virtually penniless. The little

Frankoma kiln. Sapulpa, Oklahoma, c. 1970. John Frank inspects the state-of-the-art shuttle kiln installed in 1968.

company that my ambitious father hoped would one day employ forty employees was now writing pay checks for one hundred and forty.

Although its payroll was never as large as many other companies in the state, and its dollar volume did not compare with many of the larger industries, it is believed that more people across America knew of Frankoma Pottery from Oklahoma than any other basic industry in the state, with the possible exception of the oil industry.

*F*rankoma Pottery was reaching the height of its fame, as well as its fortune. Its future never looked brighter. It had come a long way from a small charred studio in 1933, and in the summer of 1983 Frankoma's 50th Anniversary was grandly celebrated.

Barely two months later, on September 26th, history cruelly repeated itself and Frankoma again suffered the greatest tragedy of all. It was sometime around five A.M. when the night watchman smelled smoke and ran to discover a fire in the rear of the plant near the maintenance shop already spreading to the floor above. He made his way through the heavy smoke to a phone in the kiln room to call the fire department. But the outside wires had already been burned, and the phone was dead. As he was running out the door to his pickup to drive to a phone, he heard the sirens approaching. A resident across the highway had already been up, seen the flames, and made the call for help.

When Joniece and her husband arrived, the fire was beyond control and there was little to be saved. Fifty years of ceramic history had gone up in smoke. The dawn's early light revealed all that was left standing—a room at the rear of the plant and, at the front, a tall stone monolith, the fireplace that had once been a part of the beautiful Frankoma showroom. John Frank had engineered it and laid the stones himself. All else was at ground level and blackened as if a dark blanket had been respectfully placed over it. At the top of the chimney still clung the wrought iron letters

Joniece Frank. Sapulpa, Oklahoma, 1985. President and CEO of Frankoma Pottery, 1973-1991.

FRANKOMA POTTERY, like a gravestone marking the place that the once-living has been laid to rest.

Of course there was insurance. Joniece had always seen to that. But, as is so common, the plant was not insured for its replacement value.

John Frank did, however, have the foresight to create some insurance of his own. He had learned from the fire of 1938 that it was virtually impossible to begin again without the master molds. So some years before his death, he had built a fireproof mold shop to house those precious items, in the event a similar tragedy should ever occur. At least that was a blessing, even if absolutely everything else would have to be replaced and rebuilt from the ground up.

But was it worth beginning all over again? Would the public and the Frankoma family of established wholesale accounts wait the year or more it would take for Frankoma to rise again from the ashes and resume producing and shipping? Or would they go elsewhere to fill their shelves and in time forget about us? Suppose a scaled-down version of Frankoma were to be built with the insurance money; it would still require a substantial amount of borrowed capital. These were the unknowns that plagued Joniece and kept her awake nights. It was painful to think about—starting the business all over again from the beginning and resuming a heavy burden of debt that would take untold years of work and planning to climb out of.

But her real dilemma was broader and deeper than any of the above. More distressing than all else was the thought that her Frankoma family would be, in a sense, homeless. What would they do until they found employment? How would they manage? They could perhaps collect unemployment benefits for a time, but for how long? What would become of them? Some of her employees had started working part time when they were in high school and had never worked for anyone else.

The majority of Joniece's people had been there for all of twenty years or more, and several had served loyally for more than forty. Some of them were employed when slip was still being poured into molds from galvanized buckets while she played at their feet beneath the casting benches. Was it fair to "take the money and run?" The insurance settlement rightfully and legally belonged to her, but could she in all good conscience use the money for herself and slide into comfortable obscurity, while the family she grew up with and loved floundered for lack of income?

That was the real crux of it. That was the aching dilemma she faced every waking minute of every day.

Finally Joniece called a meeting of her key staff members. She needed to talk with them, learn their feelings, get their input, listen to their advice.

For a while, a portable building was used as an office. Then a small house across the highway from Frankoma was bought and furnished with second-hand desks and chairs. Of course the computers and all the vast data that had been stored in them were gone, and now typewriters and out-of-date office equipment were being used, purchased with some of the insurance money.

It can never be said that Joniece is not a woman of incredible strength. In the year prior to the fire, she had managed to get Frankoma free of all debt by working all the exhausting wholesale gift shows herself from coast to coast to keep orders coming in at maximum volume, all the while overseeing the plant's daily operations and ensuring that all orders were promptly filled and shipped. In addition, she worked late virtually every night in her studio to keep up with the task of designing new pieces and specials she had taken on.

But eventually she over-extended herself, both with her professional duties and civic activities. She hadn't taken a vacation since before she assumed leadership of the business ten years previously. She was on the verge of a physical breakdown.

And then came the fire.

Now Joniece was also emotionally exhausted from the fire's devastating toll, having watched her life's work and that of her family—for which she had labored so long and so hard to bring to its peak—perish before her eyes. And gone, too, were the many personal treasures that had once lived there, including so many of Joe Taylor and Papa's valuable early works. Only about ten percent of what had disappeared in a pillar of smoke could be replaced; all else was irreplaceable, lost forever.

She had done her homework; she had calculated rebuilding costs and tried to warn her people of the perils that lay ahead. Frankoma had never been just a building, and the construction of the plant would be the very least of the daunting task that loomed before her. She sensed the impending backbreaking struggles, and even possible failure, of such an undertaking.

But the Frankoma family was a clan of fighters—accomplishment and goal-oriented. And so, true to their courageous collective spirit, they urged that the entity be rebuilt, returned to its former glory, and they pledged to carry on as before. Joniece was tired and hadn't the strength to fight the overwhelming forces of optimism, positive they could do anything they set their minds and hands to.

And so the decision was made that Frankoma would be rebuilt and, hopefully, brought to life again. After all, they had the master molds, thanks to the foresight of the bossman. It seemed to be his intention that Frankoma should continue, else he would not have ensured the survival of those master molds.

When it came to his daughter, John Frank had been anything but a merciful task master and had always worked her harder than any of his employees, demanding that she arrive earlier and work later than all the others. He would make certain that only pure clay filled her veins. And even now, or at least it certainly seemed, the old man was still cracking the whip from wherever he was watching.

Joniece drove home, collapsed onto her bed and woke up two days later.

There was a ceremony for the presentation of the insurance check, a ceremony for the signing of the contractor, and a ceremony for the breaking of the frozen, snow-covered ground. And when there were no more ceremonies—then the real work began.

The Frankoma plant was reconstructed to dimensions only slightly larger than half its previous size. The showroom was rebuilt around the fireplace and chimney that survived.

Even at that, it turned out that Joniece's original figures were conservative. Frankoma would have to go even deeper into debt than anticipated to stay alive.

In the meantime, it seemed the whole world had heard of Frankoma's tragic destruction. Unfortunately, the news of its reconstruction and continuation had failed to reach the same ears. Most had assumed it was the end of the story and the final curtain had fallen. To this day, many surprised visitors are still heard to say, "I haven't ordered because I heard Frankoma was destroyed years ago!"

Another crippling aspect was that some of the most valuable members of her staff had suddenly reached their sixties and, one by one, were leaving Frankoma to retire. These experienced workers had proven irreplaceable, and the gaps they left behind were giant. There came a time when only a small handful of people remained whom Joniece could depend upon, those loyal ones who would not leave her in her time of need.

There was Ted Steeples who had started work at Frankoma when he was a high school boy and had filled the position of vice president and plant manager for almost as long as anyone could remember. He was also Joniece's best friend, as well as her right hand in all of the plant's operations. She often said of him, "No one in the world can fire a more perfect kiln than Ted." He was now approaching his seventies, but he would not leave Joniece and his Frankoma family.

After a time, an investor came forward with an offer to fund it's comeback, and it seemed like a good idea at the time. But there were certain conditions, some in the contract and some not, that were very difficult for Joniece and her employees to meet. But it seemed the only option, and she agreed, hoping that this would be the answer. It wasn't.

After a year, Joniece had virtually lost what little control of the company that was rightfully hers. The man had wasted much of his own money, and Frankoma was in worse shape than ever. He did not go willingly, nor did he go quietly, but he did go.

In the spring of 1990, an IRS agent entered the office and announced to Joniece that the business would have to be put on the public auction block in order to bring Frankoma's debt with them current. It mattered not in the least that timely payments were being made, nor that our father's debt to them had been more than twice that amount when he died.

Frankoma immediately filed Chapter 11 to protect itself, and the IRS did not protest, knowing that its assets far surpassed the amount of taxes due. They also saw that Joniece was sincere in her efforts to find a buyer. They would wait.

In the meantime, business, such as it was, continued. Joniece had just gone through a traumatic and heart-breaking divorce, and now she faced the loss of everything that remained of Frankoma. She resigned herself to the circumstances and began to search for prospective buyers for the business, while she succumbed to depression and an illness that would last for a very long time.

ichard Bernstein, a New England businessman, purchased Frankoma Pottery in April of 1991 for the price of its back taxes and outstanding debts. According to Chapter 11 bankruptcy laws, the new owner necessarily renamed the entity, and it became Frankoma Pottery, a Division of Frankoma Industries, Inc. A new president was installed and key positions filled with new people. Joniece was to be retained by the company.

In November of 1991, Joniece's closest friend of forty-five years died.

For all the Frankoma family, Ted Steeples represented the cornerstone of the once proud Frankoma. To some he was father, to some he was brother. In a sense he had "raised" many of them, having instilled in them the meaning of good work ethics, friendship, fairness, and loyalty. After all, it was Frankoma where Ted himself had been raised from a high school boy, and he was inspired to pass on to them many of the qualities instilled in him by the bossman. He had come to be the bossman's right hand, and it seemed there was nothing he could not do.

Ted's passing was grieved by all the Frankoma family. But for Joniece it was the end of an era. Along with all the other losses she had suffered, this was the final taking away of all she had left of the past to hold on to. But in the meantime, the world would go on, and so would Frankoma. And Joniece would stay with the company and work wherever she could prove to be an asset.

Having been apprentice to the bossman since childhood, and subsequent president of the company for almost twenty years, Joniece felt lost and detached, no longer the matriarch of her Frankoma family. Never having been an employee, it was a major transition for her to make. No longer could she prepare and serve Thanksgiving and Christmas dinners to her employees at holidays; no longer could she be involved in their personal lives, giving wedding presents to newlyweds, gifts to the newborns, and providing comfort at the deaths of close relatives; no longer would there be that close family association they had always enjoyed. The Frankoma family now belonged to someone else. She had to let them go, and they had to let her go as well. She felt estranged, alienated, and lonely.

Seven months later, Joniece collapsed. After two heart attacks in forty-eight hours, she slipped into a coma for five long days. No one knew if she would survive. But on the sixth day she finally opened her eyes. However, it was many days before she could remember what had happened to her. After a time, she was able to face up to the fact that her illness was a direct result of the misery and personal humiliation she had suffered, and was continuing to suffer, from the guilt of having lost Frankoma.

Realizing that there must have been a reason that her life had been spared, that God had kept her here for a purpose of His own, Joniece wisely sought professional help to reconstruct her life in order to continue living and dealing with all that she had been dealt.

When Joniece returned to work, she resolved to get back on her feet and prove herself. She looked around for a department that needed her, and she didn't have to look far. The retail showroom was in need of cleaning and restocking, and especially needed someone to create displays that were seasonable and timely. All this she knew well how to do, as she had been taught by Grace Lee. She immediately began working to make the showroom a shopping place customers would remember and want to return to.

Now that she was recovering and feeling somewhat better, her sense of humor was returning, and she could now laugh at herself. Here she was, back in retail where she had been when she was first put on the payroll the summer she was twelve years old! It's got to be true—what goes 'round comes 'round.

Soon Joniece realized all was not well with Mother and her husband Milton, whom she had married in 1975. They were advancing in years, and soon my sister began going to their house every day after work to make sure they were getting a nutritious meal. Each evening she cooked for them and stayed until they were in bed before she went home.

In the spring of 1993, Mother suffered a fall that left her nearly incapacitated. And both Milton's eyesight and hearing were failing fast. Then there were no choices to be made. Joniece gave up her own home and moved into theirs to care for them—all in addition to her full-time duties at Frankoma.

By autumn, Joniece was frayed and weakened from the burden of these two full-time jobs. She called me several times during those fall months, and we talked a lot. She never asked that I return and help her with the task at hand. But after a visit to see for myself, my eyes were opened wide, and then my choice had to be made as well. It was clearly a two-person job. We agreed the folks should remain at home in familiar surroundings and not be separated from their personal belongings, or each other, as long as we could care for them.

By the middle of November I had sold most of what I owned, finished wrapping up my life in Palm Springs, and moved back to Sapulpa.

The adjustment was not easy for either Joniece or me, having both lived independently for so long and having become rather set in our individual ways. And it didn't happen in a week or a month. But it did eventually evolve. We divided our duties and responsibilities and made of it an efficient and well-maintained household.

CHAPTER 23

t was summer, 1994, and Joniece and I had just been contacted by a Robert Hase, a relatively new collector of Frankoma in Belvidere, Illinois. Bob had put a small ad in the classifieds, hoping to reach other collectors with whom he could share information and do some trading. With only eight responses, he bravely started a little newsletter as an information link. When he mailed us the first issue, we immediately recognized the quality of his work, and we called him. Thus, a very pleasant friendship began via telephone.

I made a copy of Bob's newsletter and took it to our friends Tom and Jeannie Grogg, owners of Antique World, an antique mall in downtown Sapulpa. They read it, loved it, and wanted to subscribe. With a phone call to Bob, we learned that he was giving them away, and their names went on the mailing list. With us, that made twelve.

Copies of copies and more copies were made, and we began giving them to all the collectors and would-be collectors who wanted them. The Groggs, having dealt for many years with Frankoma collectors across the country, began giving away copies of the newsletter at Antique World and to their collector friends. By the second issue, the mailing list had grown significantly.

Soon Joniece, the Groggs, and I started talking about perhaps getting a few Frankoma collectors together for a day, and we wondered if we could bring together as many as twenty-five or thirty. Of course we only considered those in the immediate area, as we had no intention of making a really big to-do of it. We just thought it might be fun.

We told Bob Hase about what we intended to do, and he wrote a blurb about it in the summer edition of the newsletter, asking for a show of interest. We were flooded with inquiries! It seems those several people had told several people, and they had told several people, and before we knew it there were many more than we thought we could accommodate. We were reluctant to even mention it to another person. And we didn't dare announce it in any of the trade papers!

We scheduled the two-day event for September 17 and 18, just two months away. More than a hundred people from sixteen states and Canada wrote or called to register. We scrambled for motel rooms, listed places for them to eat, borrowed downtown parking spaces, began setting up an itinerary, and closed registration immediately.

The *Midwestern Frankoma Newsletter* had suddenly spread to several states and Canada. It was already time for a new name, and Bob Hase asked via his newsletter for suggestions. A few were offered, but none of them made anyone light up and say, "Yes, that's it!"

It wasn't until the weekend of the "First Annual Frankoma Collectors Convention" (as it had come to be known) that someone suggested the absolute perfect name. Joniece had greeted the collectors by saying, "Welcome to the Frankoma family!" An hour later, one very bright lady said, "We've already gotten so close, I feel like we really are family. Why don't we call ourselves the 'Frankoma Family?'"

That was the "that's it!" we were all looking for. Hearty applause followed, the search was over, and soon thereafter we would officially become the Frankoma Family Collectors Association.

The second floor of Antique World was set up with tables for some to show their collections, and there was a lot of buying, selling, trading, and socializing during certain hours, as well as a lot of good story telling.

A local church was kind enough to donate a bus to transport the group to locations we thought would be of interest to everyone.

There was the First Methodist Church to view the huge ceramic cross on the wall behind the pulpit, crafted and donated by John Frank when the building was consctructed in 1967. The church is also well known for its outstanding panels of stained glass windows.

There was also a visit to the mausoleum where Papa's body is interred, over which was installed a colorful and symbolic stained glass window donated by the Frankoma family of employees in honor of the bossman. In 1988, Joniece sculpted and affixed to the marble facades three miniature pottery replicas. Over the name FRANK is a small, green pacing puma in front of a ceramic pot, Frankoma's original trademark. Over the name JOHN is a small "V-4" in black and rubbed bisque, the last collector's vase designed by him. Over the name GRACE LEE is the "V-5" in the flame glaze, the following year's vase in the series, the first collector's vase designed by her.

Early in the planning, one of the first things we had decided to do was open our home to the collectors during their visit. Many had heard of the "ceramic house" designed by Bruce Goff, and some had seen photos. Now they would have a chance to view it in person.

Our own family collection was displayed throughout the house and included many of the early Frankoma pieces made at Norman, several of Joniece's original sculptures never reproduced, various one-of-a-kind works by Joseph Taylor, and pieces made by many of John Frank's contemporaries. There are also many rare and interesting pieces that are not Frankoma that were collected from every corner of the globe to which John and Grace Lee had traveled.

Although many items are irreplaceable, people were still encouraged to pick up, hold, feel, and photograph anything they wished, as that's what would have pleased Papa. He created things to be touched and handled and enjoyed for their tactile beauty, as well as visual. Some of the proudest moments of his life were when blind people came into the showroom and raved about the beauty of his work. "This," he often said, "gives me great satisfaction—to know I've made something a sightless person can love and appreciate. It's by far my highest compliment."

It pleased us to watch people wander through the house and around the outside of the structure, touching and enjoying the glazed brick and tile walls, sensing the warmth and love still retained in all that John Frank created or touched.

In the afternoon they toured the Frankoma plant. For some it was the first visit, even though they had been collectors for years, even decades.

On the second afternoon, all gathered for a formal meeting. Oklahoma State Senator Ted Fisher was master of ceremonies. Representative Mike Tyler read a personal letter from Governor David Walters, recognizing Frankoma's contributions to community and state, and officially declaring it "John and Grace Lee Frank Appreciation Day." Sapulpa Mayor John Bingham and Creek County Commissioner Dana Hudgins gave welcoming speeches as well, and all recounted fond memories of growing up with Frankoma Pottery.

Joniece Frank spoke movingly about her own successes and tragedies, both business and personal, and of her hopes and wishes for the future of Frankoma Industries.

Frankoma's new owner, Richard Bernstein, spoke of why he purchased the entity, from both business and personal standpoints. He explained many of the current problems with new government regulations that necessitated some of the many changes that were being made in its materials and manufacturing processes. The collectors were able to understand the reasons that it could never again be the Frankoma it once was, but that it must move forward with the times. The character of its products would hereafter necessarily change, as the new organization would be aiming for certain large markets heretofore untargeted by the former.

Just as the meeting was being concluded, one of the members stepped to the podium and declared that something very special and wonderful had happened in those two days, and it was proposed that the Frankoma Family become a formal organization. Within minutes, an enthusiastic group had elected officers and plans were in the making for a Frankoma Family reunion, slated for September of 1995.

Suddenly Frankoma collectors began surfacing in every part of the country in numbers no one could have suspected! And the membership roll of the organization has continued to grow from that time forward.

Incidentally, upon becoming a collector of Frankoma, one may find that a phenomenon very often discussed among collectors is regarding a certain mysterious factor that some say caused them to begin collecting Frankoma in the first place. And the experience seems to occur almost every time someone makes another rare find.

No matter how old the piece, all one needs do to feel that special something is to hold it in the hands, and the desire to take it home and own it often becomes irresistible. Strangely, the age of the piece seems to be no factor, although it's rumored that the older it is, the stronger the impulse can be felt. The sensation is often described as a voice that speaks to you without words and says, "For you, with love."

Ask for an explanation, and you're likely to hear that long ago its creator imbued it with certain qualities by loving it and honoring it, and the warmth of feelings from all those who handled it along the way were added to it to become a permanent part of its living spirit.

Is it possible that a piece of earth can actually retain all those feelings placed in it so long ago? Some collectors will argue that it's the only logical answer to the mystery. They may remind you of what John Frank said about the magical properties that clay possesses, just like the God-given divinity and potential that are ours.

So while you're enjoying your dinner some evening, take a moment to appreciate the Frankoma plate on which it is being served. Or as you sip your coffee from a sturdy Frankoma cup or mug, think of all that went into the creation of the piece you hold in your hand.

Be reminded that once upon a time it was a seemingly worthless piece of dirt sitting on a hill, unnoticed and unappreciated. But one day the master came along and saw it, and he knew it wasn't just dirt.

He alone recognized it to be that special living substance called "clay," with all its unique qualities and limitless potential.

And he said, "Come with me. Let me make you into something of beauty and value, so that you may serve my brothers and sisters." John Frank said that if anyone truly desires to become that something of beauty and service to benefit mankind, all that is required is that you fully trust that it is possible, then surrender your will to the Master's will, and become as clay in His hands.

And so the new Frankoma Industries will continue on into the new century in its own new direction, with new and different products and designs, many of which are now generated on a computer. (Many exceptions are those items of sculpture that Joniece Frank is and will be designing, now that she has been assigned to do what she does best—creating meaningful art that people relate to and want to live with.)

But be assured that the Frankoma Pottery of John and Grace Lee and Joniece Frank is very much alive today, thanks to the devoted members of the new Frankoma Family Collectors Association. The earlier works of these artists are now enjoying a rich afterlife that will allow them to be treasured for lifetimes as they are handed down from present to future generations.

It is true that many of the current collectors are in their senior years. But how very satisfying it is to look around and see the many young people who are becoming avid collectors as well. And their children will be educated as to the beauty and value of the Frankoma Pottery that will one day be theirs. If flea markets and antique malls and yard sales still exist when those children become adults, surely they will be out there on weekends doing precisely what their ancestors did— looking for rare pieces of Frankoma that were once mere clay in one of these masters' hands.

And they will be attending Frankoma Family reunions year after year to meet with other collectors with whom they will bargain, trade, swap stories, laugh, and enjoy the rich and rewarding friendships that are bound to evolve. And as their mentors taught them, so will they become the teachers of the next generation of Frankoma collectors.

John Frank was apparently right when he said, "Things of quality have no fear of time."

A Giant Among Men

The Man that I married
Is a giant among men.
His heart is so big
It leaps out of him,
Then reaches out to the young
With a kind, loving word
And points them to God
When their visions are blurred.

His artistic hands
Can build mansions with mud,
Or he'll fight for a cause
With his last drop of blood.
There are no chores
He will not attend;
He may fix the kitchen sink
Or my diamond ring mend.
His God is his guide,
People are his love.
When he faces trouble
He asks help from above.

He's a giant among men,
He's my lover, my life.
I thank God every day
That I am his wife.

GRACE LEE FRANK
February 1972

race Lee's story deserves a book all its own, as her own personal accomplishments have placed her name in such volumes of honor as *The First Fifty Years of Oklahoma*, *Outstanding Personalities of the South*, *International Biography of Contemporary Achievements 1975*, and *Notables of the Bicentennial Era*, to mention a few. She was also chosen to join the rolls of *Who's Who in Oklahoma* and *Who's Who in America*.

Grace Lee Frank Smith. 1977.

Reverend A. Milton Smith, and his wife Opal, had remained close friends with John and Grace Lee Frank for more than forty-five years. Opal passed away just one year before Papa.

One day in January of 1975, Milton was traveling through Sapulpa and, as always, stopped to say hello. He and Grace Lee were happily married one month later.

Grace Lee maintained her position as Executive Vice President of Frankoma Pottery and continued until 1983 to serve on the Board of Directors in an advisory capacity, after which she retired.

In 1982, a book of her inspirational poetry was published titled, *Look Up and Smile*.

She continues to live in "the house built like a smile" in Sapulpa.

The Jim Thorpe Medal,
front and back.

*F*ollowing the example of her mentor, Joniece came to be equally as active in community and state affairs as our father had been. In 1971 she created the Jim Thorpe Award trophy which, for several years thereafter, was presented to the Outstanding Oklahoma High School Athlete.

In addition, she designed and created an outstanding Jim Thorpe commemorative medal which was struck in both silver and bronze at the U.S. Mint in Philadelphia. Being both a ceramic designer and moldmaker, Joniece knew well the crucial dynamics of creating objects so that a mold can easily be pulled from them. She became the first artist in American history to design a medal struck at the U.S. Mint whose final model (a replica two feet in diameter) did not necessitate a Mint craftsman to rework or alter it in any way prior to its reproduction.

Elected to the board of directors of the Oklahoma Athletic Hall of Fame, she was also a member of the Jim Thorpe Committee beginning in 1971, and in 1975 was appointed by Governor David Boren to the Jim Thorpe Commission.

Joniece served on the boards of directors of the Women's Chamber of Commerce, the Sapulpa Chamber of Commerce and Sapulpa Recreation, Inc.

She also served on the board of directors of the Tulsa chapter of Executives' Secretaries, Inc.; was vice president of the TLC School for Retarded Children; was one of four selected business people to annually judge and award the outstanding Junior Achievement Club of the year; served on the Tulsa Educational Advisory Committee; and was a member of the Industrial Executives Council of the Metropolitan Tulsa Chamber of Commerce.

Joniece Frank became the first woman to be accepted into the membership of the exclusive Tulsa Area Manufacturers Club, subsequently voted to its board of directors, and in 1975-76 became the first woman to hold the office of president.

In 1975 she was voted Executive of the Year for the City of Tulsa. 1976 brought her the honor of being chosen Outstanding Woman Executive in the State of Oklahoma.

Joniece is currently retained by the new owner of Frankoma to design a limited number of art pieces. Her latest work is a series of angels.

*M*y story? To be sure, not nearly as illustrious or significant as those above. I was an actress and singer for fifteen years in New York, California, and several points between, and sometimes toured with night club shows and musical reviews as a featured singer. I've also worked as a clown, a public stenographer, an executive secretary, a massage therapist, a word processer, a free-lance writer, and sales representative for Cynthia Ferrari Designs. I based myself in Los Angeles for the better part of thirty-five years, and the last four years in sunny Palm Springs, California.

Donna Frank. 1995.

In addition to the eight countries in Europe that summer with my family, I've since traveled to Egypt, Israel, Jordan, India, Nepal, to Surinam (South America) via freighter, Santo Domingo, the Bahamas, and spent a month in a Shingon Buddhist monastery on a mountain top in Japan, all just for fun, pleasure, and adventure.

Did I write all I said I would? Yes. Has any of it been published? No. What I wrote was truth when I wrote it, but by the time I finished, what I had written was no longer true. Because a time came when the real Truth made itself known to me, and for that there are no words I can put on paper.

In November of 1993, I moved back to Sapulpa to help my sister take care of our mother and the house. When the Frankoma Family Collectors Association came into being, somehow (it's still not clear to me how it happened) I was elected secretary. So I still do a lot of writing—letters, letters, I write letters! I also contribute articles now and then to FFCA's *Pot & Puma* and the *Prairie Green Sheet*.

I am an admitted logophile, a lover of malaprops, spoonerisms, and serendipity, and a devoted fan of Calvin and Hobbes, the Los Angeles Dodgers, and the Sunday *LA Times* crossword puzzles.

Now that I'm winding up this second edition of *Clay*, am I planning anymore books? No commitments, only a semidefinite "maybe," in that I'm toying with the idea of compiling and evaporating on some of my travel stories, which promises to be a right funful project.

Beyond that, my crystal ball is still pretty foggy.

FRANKOMA FAMILY COLLECTORS ASSOCIATION

Charter Year 1995

Come join us!

Dues: $20 per year

Quarterly Newsletters, Quarterly Classified Ads,
Discounts from Frankoma Pottery, Annual Convention & More.

To join the Frankoma Family Collectors Association and receive your subscription to *Pot and Puma* and *Prairie Green Sheet*, fill out the form below and mail it along with your check to FFCA Treasurer, Nancy L. Littrell, P.O. Box 32571, Oklahoma City, OK 73123-0771. *Make checks payable to: FFCA*

Name/Names

Address

City   State Zip + 4 digit code   Area code & telephone

What type of Frankoma do you collect? (miniature, sculpture, glaze, Ada, S&P, etc.)

Please list any hobby or skill (photography, computer, writing, editing, publicity, bookkeeping, auctioning, art, etc.) **you would be willing to volunteer.**

FFCA publishes an annual membership directory. Please indicate your preferred listing:

    ❑ Complete listing as presented above
    ❑ Full address, omit phone
    ❑ Name and city only
    ❑ Do not list my name, address, or telephone